UK

NINJA DUAL ZONE AIR FRYER

Cookbook 2024

Super Easy & Effortless Air Fryer Recipes, Crispy and Nutritious Family Meals for Beginners| Dual Zone Air Frying | UK Measurements

Carol J. Powe

We sincerely appreciate your respect for the author's work and copyright. We hope you savor your culinary journey with this recipe book!

CONTENTS

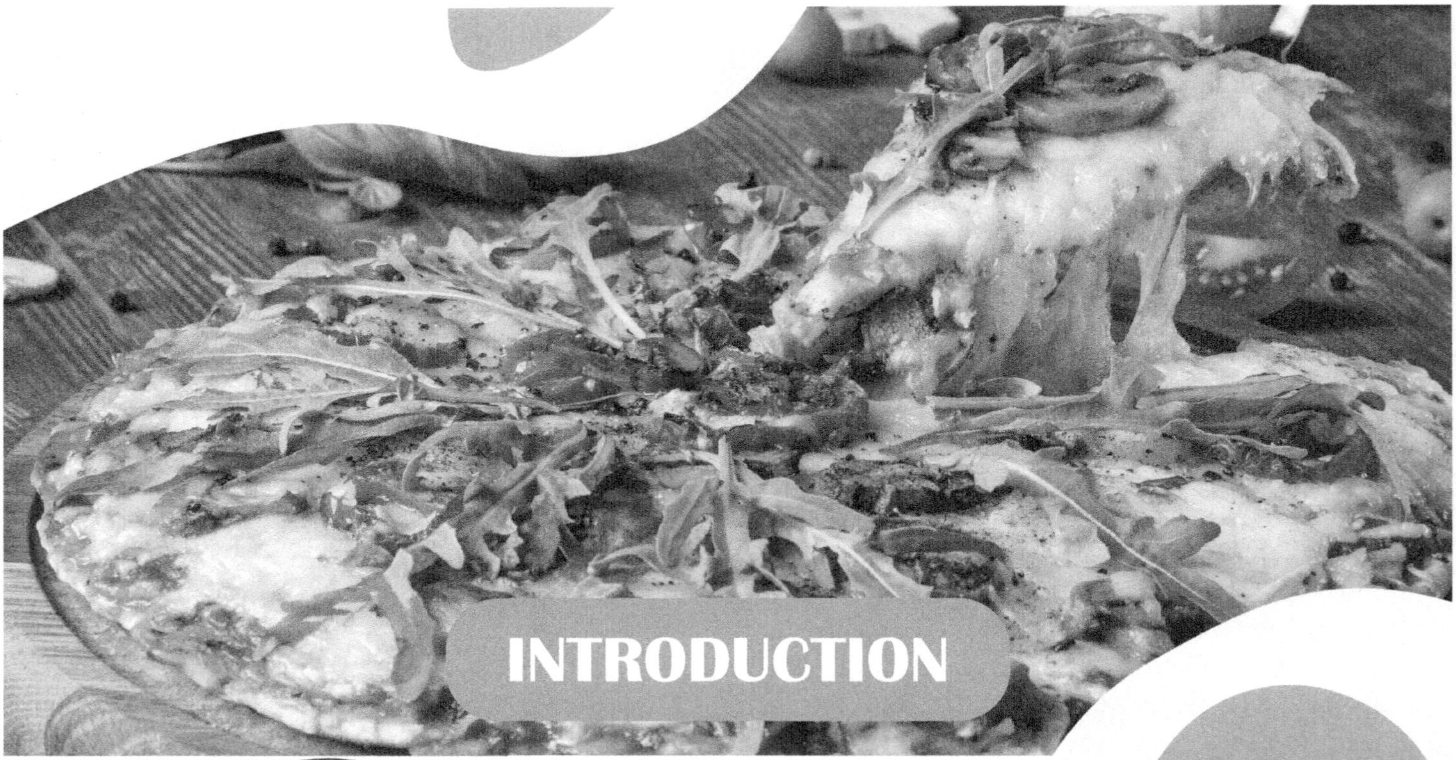

INTRODUCTION

Greetings, culinary adventurers! I'm Carol J. Powe, and I'm thrilled to introduce you to the culinary wonderland that is my Ninja Dual Zone Air Fryer Cookbook. Picture a world where cooking is not a chore but a delightful journey filled with mouth-watering discoveries. That's the world I want to invite you into.

My own culinary odyssey began with a love for creating dishes that not only tantalize the taste buds but also warm the heart. From my humble beginnings as a home cook to my role as a culinary educator, I've seen firsthand the joy that great food can bring to people's lives.

The heart and soul of this cookbook lie in its mission—to make cooking accessible, exciting, and downright fun. The Ninja Dual Zone Air Fryer is a kitchen wizard, and together, we'll unleash its magic. In these pages, you'll find a treasure trove of recipes, each one a carefully crafted masterpiece that brings out the best in this incredible appliance.

Whether you're a seasoned kitchen maestro or someone taking their first steps into the culinary world, my cookbook has something for you. With step-by-step instructions that are as friendly as a chat with a fellow food lover, you'll be whipping up gourmet delights in no time. And those handy shopping lists? They're your secret weapon to stress-free grocery runs. Plus, I've tailored every cooking time to suit the Ninja Dual Zone Air Fryer's tempo, and I've sprinkled in practical tips and tricks like confetti at a celebration.

My deepest hope is that this cookbook becomes your trusty sidekick in the kitchen, elevating your cooking game, and turning mealtime into a culinary adventure. It's about creating unforgettable moments and dishes that linger in your memory.

So, open these pages and embrace the world of the Ninja Dual Zone Air Fryer. Let's embark on a gastronomic journey together—one filled with flavor, creativity, and the sheer joy of cooking.

Happy cooking, my fellow food explorers!

Carol J. Powe

FEATURES OF DUAL ZONE AIR FRYER

Dual Cooking Zones: Two independent cooking areas.

Versatility: Cook diverse foods simultaneously.

Time-Saving: Reduce overall meal preparation time.

Customization: Individual temperature and time controls.

Efficient: Energy-saving, single-appliance cooking.

Large Capacity: Suitable for multiple servings.

BENEFITS OF AIR FRYER COOKING

- **Reduced Fat Consumption**

Air fryer cooking significantly reduces the amount of oil required to achieve crispy results. Traditional deep-frying can saturate food with unhealthy fats, while air frying typically uses just a fraction of the oil. This translates to lower overall fat intake, which can contribute to better heart health and weight management.

- **Lower Calorie Content**

With less oil used in air frying, the calorie content of meals is also reduced. This can be beneficial for individuals looking to control their calorie intake and manage their weight. Enjoying favorite fried foods with fewer calories can make a positive impact on overall dietary habits.

- **Less Acrylamide Formation**

When starchy foods like potatoes are fried at high temperatures, they can produce acrylamide, a potentially harmful chemical. Air frying at lower temperatures reduces the risk of acrylamide formation, making air-fried foods a safer choice compared to deep-fried alternatives.

- **Healthier Cooking Method**

Air fryers cook food by circulating hot air around it, which retains more of the food's natural moisture. This cooking method preserves nutrients and flavor, resulting in healthier and tastier dishes. It's a great way to enjoy vegetables and proteins without overcooking or nutrient loss.

- **Minimized Risk of Harmful Compounds**

Deep-frying at high temperatures can lead to the formation of harmful compounds like trans fats and oxidation products. Air frying operates at lower temperatures, reducing the risk of creating these unhealthy substances. This makes air-fried foods a safer and more health-conscious choice.

WHAT KIND OF FOOD CAN AIR FRYER BE USED TO COOK?

- Frozen items like fries and nuggets.

- Proteins like wings and steak.

- Vegetables, maintaining crunch.

- Baked goods.

- Appetizers and snacks.

- Desserts like churros.

- Reheating leftovers.

CLEANING TIPS FOR AIR FRYER

Cool Down: Always allow your air fryer to cool down before cleaning to avoid burns.

Remove and Clean Removable Parts: Take out the cooking basket, tray, and other removable parts. Wash them with warm, soapy water or place them in the dishwasher if they are dishwasher-safe.

Wipe Down the Interior: Use a damp cloth to wipe down the interior of the air fryer, removing any food particles or residue.

Clean the Heating Element: Carefully clean the heating element or coil and the fan using a brush or a soft, damp cloth. Ensure they are free from grease or debris.

Empty Oil Tray: If your air fryer has an oil collection tray, empty and clean it regularly to prevent buildup. Dispose of excess oil properly.

Check the Air Vent: Ensure that the air vent or venting system is clean and free of any obstructions for proper ventilation.

BREAKFAST RECIPES

Breakfast Recipes

Breakfast Casserole

Servings:4 | Cooking Time:10

Ingredients:

- 1 pound of beef sausage, grounded
- 1/4 cup diced white onion
- 1 diced green bell pepper
- 8 whole eggs, beaten
- ½ cup Colby jack cheese, shredded
- ¼ teaspoon of garlic salt
- Oil spray, for greasing

Directions:

1. Take a bowl and add ground sausage to it.
2. Add in the diced onions, bell peppers, eggs and whisk it well.
3. Then season it with garlic salt.
4. Spray both the baskets of the air fryer with oil spray.
5. Divide this mixture among the baskets; remember to remove the crisper plates.
6. Top the mixture with cheese.
7. Now, turn ON the Ninja Foodie 2-Basket Air Fryer zone 1 and select AIR FRY mode and set the time to 10 minutes at 390 degrees F.
8. Select the MATCH button for zone 2 baskets, and hit start.
9. Once the cooking cycle completes, take out, and serve.
10. Serve and enjoy.

Nutrition Info:

- (Per serving) Calories 699| Fat 59.1g | Sodium 1217 mg | Carbs 6.8g | Fiber 0.6g| Sugar 2.5g | Protein33.1 g

Breakfast Potatoes

Servings: 6 | Cooking Time: 20 Minutes

Ingredients:

- 3 potatoes, peeled and diced
- 1 onion yellow, diced
- 1 green pepper diced
- 2 teaspoons salt
- ½ teaspoon pepper
- 2 tablespoons olive oil
- 1 cup cheese shredded

Directions:

1. Toss potatoes with onion, green peppers, black pepper, salt and cheese in a bowl.
2. Divide the potato mixture into the Ninja Foodi 2 Baskets Air Fryer baskets.
3. Return the air fryer basket 1 to Zone 1, and basket 2 to Zone 2 of the Ninja Foodi 2-Basket Air Fryer.
4. Choose the "Air Fry" mode for Zone 1 at 400 degrees F temperature and 20 minutes of cooking time.
5. Select the "MATCH COOK" option to copy the settings for Zone 2.
6. Initiate cooking by pressing the START/PAUSE BUTTON.
7. Toss the veggies once cooked halfway through.
8. Serve warm.

Nutrition Info:

- (Per serving) Calories 209 | Fat 7.5g |Sodium 321mg | Carbs 34.1g | Fiber 4g | Sugar 3.8g | Protein 4.3g

Egg White Muffins

Servings: 8 | Cooking Time: 10 Minutes

Ingredients:

- 4 slices center-cut bacon, cut into strips
- 4 ounces baby bella mushrooms, roughly chopped
- 2 ounces sun-dried tomatoes
- 2 tablespoon sliced black olives
- 2 tablespoons grated or shredded parmesan
- 2 tablespoons shredded mozzarella
- ¼ teaspoon black pepper
- ¾ cup liquid egg whites
- 2 tablespoons liquid egg whites

Directions:

1. Heat a saucepan with a little oil, add the bacon and mushrooms and cook until fully cooked and crispy, about 6–8 minutes.
2. While the bacon and mushrooms cook, mix the ¾ cup liquid egg whites, sun-dried tomato, olives, parmesan, mozzarella, and black pepper together in a large bowl.
3. Add the cooked bacon and mushrooms to the tomato and olive mixture, stirring everything together.
4. Spoon the mixture into muffin molds, followed by 2 tablespoons of egg whites over the top.
5. Place half the muffins mold in zone 1 and half in zone 2, then insert the drawers into the unit.
6. Select zone 1, select AIR FRY, set temperature to 390 degrees F/ 200 degrees C, and set time to 22 minutes.
7. Select MATCH to match zone 2 settings to zone 1.

Press the START/STOP button to begin cooking.
8. When cooking is complete, remove the molds and enjoy!

Nutrition Info:

- (Per serving) Calories 104 | Fat 5.6g | Sodium 269mg | Carbs 3.5g | Fiber 0.8g | Sugar 0.3g | Protein 10.3g

Pepper Egg Cups

Servings: 4 | Cooking Time: 18 Minutes.

Ingredients:

- 2 halved bell pepper, seeds removed
- 4 eggs
- 1 teaspoon olive oil
- 1 pinch salt and black pepper
- 1 pinch sriracha flakes

Directions:

1. Slice the bell peppers in half, lengthwise, and remove their seeds and the inner portion to get a cup-like shape.
2. Rub olive oil on the edges of the bell peppers.
3. Place them in the two crisper plates with their cut side up and crack 1 egg in each half of bell pepper.
4. Drizzle salt, black pepper, and sriracha flakes on top of the eggs.
5. Return the crisper plates to the Ninja Foodi Dual Zone Air Fryer.
6. Choose the Air Fry mode for Zone 1 and set the temperature to 390 degrees F and the time to 18 minutes.
7. Select the "MATCH" button to copy the settings for Zone 2.
8. Initiate cooking by pressing the START/STOP button.
9. Serve warm and fresh.

Nutrition Info:

- (Per serving) Calories 183 | Fat 15g |Sodium 402mg | Carbs 2.5g | Fiber 0.4g | Sugar 1.1g | Protein 10g

Breakfast Cheese Sandwich

Servings: 2 | Cooking Time: 8 Minutes

Ingredients:

- 4 bread slices
- 2 provolone cheese slice
- ¼ tsp dried basil
- 2 tbsp mayonnaise
- 2 Monterey jack cheese slice
- 2 cheddar cheese slice
- ¼ tsp dried oregano

Directions:

1. In a small bowl, mix mayonnaise, basil, and oregano.
2. Spread mayonnaise on one side of the two bread slices.
3. Top two bread slices with cheddar cheese, provolone cheese, Monterey jack cheese slice, and cover with remaining bread slices.
4. Insert a crisper plate in the Ninja Foodi air fryer baskets.
5. Place sandwiches in both baskets.
6. Select zone 1, then select "air fry" mode and set the temperature to 390 degrees F for 8 minutes. Press "match" to match zone 2 settings to zone 1. Press "start/stop" to begin. Turn halfway through.

Nutrition Info:

- (Per serving) Calories 421 | Fat 30.7g |Sodium 796mg | Carbs 13.9g | Fiber 0.5g | Sugar 2.2g | Protein 22.5g

Sweet Potato Sausage Hash

Servings: 4 | Cooking Time: 20 Minutes

Ingredients:

- 1½ pounds sweet potato, peeled and diced into ½-inch pieces
- 1 tablespoon minced garlic
- 1 teaspoon kosher salt plus more, as desired
- Ground black pepper, as desired
- 2 tablespoons canola oil
- 1 tablespoon dried sage
- 1-pound uncooked mild ground breakfast sausage
- ½ large onion, peeled and diced
- ½ teaspoon ground cinnamon
- 1 teaspoon chili powder
- 4 large eggs, poached or fried (optional)

Directions:

1. Toss the sweet potatoes with the garlic, salt, pepper, and canola oil in a mixing bowl.
2. Install the crisper plate in the zone 1 drawer, fill it with the sweet potato mixture, and insert the drawer in the unit.
3. Place the ground sausage in the zone 2 drawer (without the crisper plate) and place it in the unit.
4. Select zone 1, then AIR FRY, and set the temperature to 400 degrees F/ 200 degrees C with a 30-minute timer.
5. Select zone 2, then ROAST, then set the temperature to 400 degrees F/ 200 degrees C with a 20-minute timer. SYNC is the option to choose. To begin cooking, press the START/STOP button.
6. When the zone 1 and zone 2 times have reached

10 minutes, press START/STOP and remove the drawers from the unit. Shake each for 10 seconds.

7. Half of the sage should be added to the zone 1 drawer.

8. Add the onion to the zone 2 drawer and mix to incorporate. To continue cooking, press START/STOP and reinsert the drawers.

9. Remove both drawers from the unit once the cooking is finished and add the potatoes to the sausage mixture. Mix in the cinnamon, sage, chili powder, and salt until thoroughly combined.

10. When the hash is done, stir it and serve it right away with a poached or fried egg on top, if desired.

Nutrition Info:

- (Per serving) Calories 491 | Fat 19.5g | Sodium 736mg | Carbs 51g | Fiber 8g | Sugar 2g | Protein 26.3

Buttermilk Biscuits With Roasted Stone Fruit Compote

Servings:4 | Cooking Time: 20 Minutes

Ingredients:

- FOR THE BISCUITS
- 1⅓ cups all-purpose flour
- 2 teaspoons sugar
- 2 teaspoons baking powder
- ½ teaspoon baking soda
- ½ teaspoon kosher salt
- 4 tablespoons (½ stick) very cold unsalted butter
- ½ cup plus 1 tablespoon low-fat buttermilk
- FOR THE FRUIT COMPOTE
- 2 peaches, peeled and diced
- 2 plums, peeled and diced
- ¼ cup water
- 2 teaspoons honey
- ⅛ teaspoon ground ginger (optional)

Directions:

1. To prep the biscuits: In a small bowl, combine the flour, sugar, baking powder, baking soda, and salt. Using the large holes on a box grater, grate in the butter. Stir in the buttermilk to form a thick dough.

2. Place the dough on a lightly floured surface and gently pat it into a ½-inch-thick disc. Fold the dough in half, then rotate the whole thing 90 degrees, pat into a ½-inch thick disc and fold again. Repeat until you have folded the dough four times.

3. Pat the dough out a final time into a ½-inch-thick disc and use a 3-inch biscuit cutter to cut 4 biscuits from the dough (discard the scraps).

4. To prep the fruit compote: In a large bowl, stir together the peaches, plums, water, honey, and ginger (if using).

5. To cook the biscuits and compote: Install a crisper plate in the Zone 1 basket, place the biscuits in the basket, and insert the basket in the unit. Place the fruit in the Zone 2 basket and insert the basket in the unit.

6. Select Zone 1, select AIR FRY, set the temperature to 400°F, and set the time to 10 minutes.

7. Select Zone 2, select ROAST, set the temperature to 350°F, and set the time to 20 minutes. Select SMART FINISH.

8. Press START/PAUSE to begin cooking.

9. When the Zone 2 timer reads 10 minutes, press START/PAUSE. Remove the basket and stir the compote. Reinsert the basket and press START/PAUSE to resume cooking.

10. When cooking is complete, the biscuits will be golden brown and crisp on top and the fruit will be soft. Transfer the biscuits to a plate to cool. Lightly mash the fruit to form a thick, jammy sauce.

11. Split the biscuits in half horizontally and serve topped with fruit compote.

Nutrition Info:

- (Per serving) Calories: 332; Total fat: 12g; Saturated fat: 7.5g; Carbohydrates: 50g; Fiber: 2.5g; Protein: 6g; Sodium: 350mg

Air Fryer Sausage Patties

Servings: 12 | Cooking Time: 10 Minutes

Ingredients:

- 1-pound pork sausage or ready-made patties
- Fennel seeds or preferred seasonings

Directions:

1. Prepare the sausage by slicing it into patties, then flavor it with fennel seed or your favorite seasonings.

2. Install a crisper plate in both drawers. Place half the patties in zone 1 and half in zone 2, then insert the drawers into the unit.

3. Select zone 1, select AIR FRY, set temperature to 390 degrees F/ 200 degrees C, and set time to 10 minutes.

4. Select MATCH to match zone 2 settings to zone 1.

5. Press the START/STOP button to begin cooking.

6. When cooking is complete, remove the patties from the unit and serve with sauce or make a burger.

Nutrition Info:

- (Per serving) Calories 130 | Fat 10.5g | Sodium 284mg | Carbs 0.3g | Fiber 0.2g | Sugar 0g | Protein 7.4g

Crispy Hash Browns

Servings: 4 | Cooking Time: 13 Minutes.

Ingredients:

- 3 russet potatoes
- ¼ cup chopped green peppers
- ¼ cup chopped red peppers
- ¼ cup chopped onions
- 2 garlic cloves chopped
- 1 teaspoon paprika
- Salt and black pepper, to taste
- 2 teaspoons olive oil

Directions:

1. Peel and grate all the potatoes with the help of a cheese grater.
2. Add potato shreds to a bowl filled with cold water and leave it soaked for 25 minutes.
3. Drain the water and place the potato shreds on a plate lined with a paper towel.
4. Transfer the shreds to a dry bowl and add olive oil, paprika, garlic, and black pepper.
5. Make four flat patties out of the potato mixture and place two into each of the crisper plate.
6. Return the crisper plate to the Ninja Foodi Dual Zone Air Fryer.
7. Choose the Air Fry mode for Zone 1 and set the temperature to 390 degrees F and set the time to 13 minutes.
8. Select the "MATCH" button to copy the settings for Zone 2.
9. Initiate cooking by pressing the START/STOP button.
10. Flip the potato hash browns once cooked halfway through, then resume cooking.
11. Once done, serve warm.

Nutrition Info:

- (Per serving) Calories 190 | Fat 18g |Sodium 150mg | Carbs 0.6g | Fiber 0.4g | Sugar 0.4g | Protein 7.2g

Sweet Potatoes Hash

Servings:2 | Cooking Time:25

Ingredients:

- 450 grams sweet potatoes
- 1/2 white onion, diced
- 3 tablespoons of olive oil
- 1 teaspoon smoked paprika
- 1/4 teaspoon cumin
- 1/3 teaspoon of ground turmeric
- 1/4 teaspoon of garlic salt
- 1 cup guacamole

Directions:

1. Peel and cut the potatoes into cubes.
2. Now, transfer the potatoes to a bowl and add oil, white onions, cumin, paprika, turmeric, and garlic salt.
3. Put this mixture between both the baskets of the Ninja Foodie 2-Basket Air Fryer.
4. Set it to AIR FRY mode for 10 minutes at 390 degrees F.
5. Then take out the baskets and shake them well.
6. Then again set time to 15 minutes at 390 degrees F.
7. Once done, serve it with guacamole.

Nutrition Info:

- (Per serving) Calories691 | Fat 49.7g| Sodium 596mg | Carbs 64g | Fiber15g | Sugar 19g | Protein 8.1g

Vanilla Strawberry Doughnuts

Servings: 8 | Cooking Time: 15 Minutes

Ingredients:

- 1 egg
- ½ cup strawberries, diced
- 80ml cup milk
- 1 tsp cinnamon
- 1 tsp baking soda
- 136g all-purpose flour
- 2 tsp vanilla
- 2 tbsp butter, melted
- 73g sugar
- ½ tsp salt

Directions:

1. In a bowl, mix flour, cinnamon, baking soda, sugar, and salt.
2. In a separate bowl, whisk egg, milk, butter, and vanilla.
3. Pour egg mixture into the flour mixture and mix until well combined.
4. Add strawberries and mix well.
5. Pour batter into the silicone doughnut moulds.
6. Insert a crisper plate in the Ninja Foodi air fryer baskets.
7. Place doughnut moulds in both baskets.
8. Select zone 1, then select "air fry" mode and set the temperature to 320 degrees F for 15 minutes. Press "match" to match zone 2 settings to zone 1. Press "start/stop" to begin.

Nutrition Info:

- (Per serving) Calories 133 | Fat 3.8g |Sodium 339mg | Carbs 21.9g | Fiber 0.8g | Sugar 9.5g | Protein 2.7g

Sausage Breakfast Casserole

Servings: 4 | Cooking Time: 10 Minutes

Ingredients:

- 455g hash browns
- 455g ground breakfast sausage
- 1 green capsicum diced
- 1 red capsicum diced
- 1 yellow capsicum diced
- ¼ cup sweet onion diced
- 4 eggs

Directions:

1. Layer each air fryer basket with parchment paper.
2. Place the hash browns in both the baskets.
3. Spread sausage, onion and peppers over the hash brown.
4. Return the air fryer basket 1 to Zone 1, and basket 2 to Zone 2 of the Ninja Foodi 2-Basket Air Fryer.
5. Choose the "Air Fry" mode for Zone 1 at 355 degrees F temperature and 10 minutes of cooking time.
6. Select the "MATCH COOK" option to copy the settings for Zone 2.
7. Initiate cooking by pressing the START/PAUSE BUTTON.
8. Beat eggs in a bowl and pour over the air fried veggies.
9. Continue air frying for 10 minutes.
10. Garnish with salt and black pepper.
11. Serve warm.

Nutrition Info:

- (Per serving) Calories 267 | Fat 12g |Sodium 165mg | Carbs 39g | Fiber 1.4g | Sugar 22g | Protein 3.3g

Breakfast Sausage Omelet

Servings:2 | Cooking Time:8

Ingredients:

- ¼ pound breakfast sausage, cooked and crumbled
- 4 eggs, beaten
- ½ cup pepper Jack cheese blend
- 2 tablespoons green bell pepper, sliced
- 1 green onion, chopped
- 1 pinch cayenne pepper
- Cooking spray

Directions:

1. Take a bowl and whisk eggs in it along with crumbled sausage, pepper Jack cheese, green onions, red bell pepper, and cayenne pepper.
2. Mix it all well.
3. Take two cake pans that fit inside the air fryer and grease it with oil spray.
4. Divide the omelet mixture between cake pans.
5. Put the cake pans inside both of the Ninja Foodie 2-Basket Air Fryer baskets.
6. Turn on the BAKE function of the zone 1 basket and let it cook for 15-20 minutes at 310 degrees F.
7. Select MATCH button for zone 2 basket.
8. Once the cooking cycle completes, take out, and serve hot, as a delicious breakfast.

Nutrition Info:

- (Per serving) Calories 691| Fat52.4g | Sodium1122 mg | Carbs 13.3g | Fiber 1.8g| Sugar 7g | Protein 42g

Egg With Baby Spinach

Servings:4 | Cooking Time:12

Ingredients:

- Nonstick spray, for greasing ramekins
- 2 tablespoons olive oil
- 6 ounces baby spinach
- 2 garlic cloves, minced
- 1/3 teaspoon kosher salt
- 6-8 large eggs
- ½ cup half and half
- Salt and black pepper, to taste
- 8 Sourdough bread slices, toasted

Directions:

1. Grease 4 ramekins with oil spray and set aside for further use.
2. Take a skillet and heat oil in it.
3. Then cook spinach for 2 minutes and add garlic and salt black pepper.
4. Let it simmer for2more minutes.
5. Once the spinach is wilted, transfer it to a plate.
6. Whisk an egg into a small bowl.
7. Add in the spinach.
8. Whisk it well and then pour half and half.
9. Divide this mixture between 4 ramekins and remember not to overfill it to the top, leave a little space on top.
10. Put the ramekins in zone 1 and zone 2 baskets of the Ninja Foodie 2-Basket Air Fryer.
11. Press start and set zone 1 to AIR fry it at 350 degrees F for 8-12 minutes.
12. Press the MATCH button for zone 2.
13. Once it's cooked and eggs are done, serve with sourdough bread slices.

Nutrition Info:

- (Per serving) Calories 404| Fat 19.6g| Sodium 761mg | Carbs 40.1g | Fiber 2.5g| Sugar 2.5g | Protein 19.2g

Breakfast Frittata

Servings: 4 | Cooking Time: 12 Minutes

Ingredients:

- 4 eggs
- 4 tablespoons milk
- 35g cheddar cheese grated
- 50g feta crumbled
- 1 tomato, deseeded and chopped
- 15g spinach chopped
- 1 tablespoon fresh herbs, chopped
- 2 spring onion chopped
- Salt and black pepper, to taste
- ½ teaspoon olive oil

Directions:

1. Beat eggs with milk in a bowl and stir in the rest of the ingredients.
2. Grease two small-sized springform pans and line them with parchment paper.
3. Divide the egg mixture into the pans and place one in each air fryer basket.
4. Return the air fryer basket 1 to Zone 1, and basket 2 to Zone 2 of the Ninja Foodi 2-Basket Air Fryer.
5. Choose the "Air Fry" mode for Zone 1 at 350 degrees F and 12 minutes of cooking time.
6. Select the "MATCH COOK" option to copy the settings for Zone 2.
7. Initiate cooking by pressing the START/PAUSE BUTTON.
8. Serve warm.

Nutrition Info:

- (Per serving) Calories 273 | Fat 22g |Sodium 517mg | Carbs 3.3g | Fiber 0.2g | Sugar 1.4g | Protein 16.1g

Perfect Cinnamon Toast

Servings: 6 | Cooking Time: 10 Minutes

Ingredients:

- 12 slices whole-wheat bread
- 1 stick butter, room temperature
- ½ cup white sugar
- 1½ teaspoons ground cinnamon
- 1½ teaspoons pure vanilla extract
- 1 pinch kosher salt
- 2 pinches freshly ground black pepper (optional)

Directions:

1. Mash the softened butter with a fork or the back of a spoon in a bowl. Add the sugar, cinnamon, vanilla, and salt. Stir until everything is well combined.
2. Spread one-sixth of the mixture onto each slice of bread, making sure to cover the entire surface.
3. Install a crisper plate in both drawers. Place half the bread sliced in the zone 1 drawer and half in the zone 2 drawer, then insert the drawers into the unit.
4. Select zone 1, select AIR FRY, set temperature to 400 degrees F/ 200 degrees C, and set time to 5 minutes. Select MATCH to match zone 2 settings to zone 1. Press theSTART/STOP button to begin cooking
5. When cooking is complete, remove the slices and cut them diagonally.
6. Serve immediately.

Nutrition Info:

- (Per serving) Calories 322 | Fat 16.5g | Sodium 249mg | Carbs 39.3g | Fiber 4.2g | Sugar 18.2g | Protein 8.2g

Breakfast Stuffed Peppers

Servings: 4 | Cooking Time: 13 Minutes

Ingredients:

- 2 capsicums, halved, seeds removed
- 4 eggs
- 1 teaspoon olive oil
- 1 pinch salt and pepper
- 1 pinch sriracha flakes

Directions:

1. Cut each capsicum in half and place two halves in each air fryer basket.
2. Crack one egg into each capsicum and top it with black pepper, salt, sriracha flakes and olive oil.
3. Return the air fryer basket 1 to Zone 1, and basket 2 to Zone 2 of the Ninja Foodi 2-Basket Air Fryer.
4. Choose the "Air Fry" mode for Zone 1 at 390 degrees F and 13 minutes of cooking time.
5. Select the "MATCH COOK" option to copy the settings for Zone 2.
6. Initiate cooking by pressing the START/PAUSE BUTTON.
7. Serve warm.

Nutrition Info:

- (Per serving) Calories 237 | Fat 19g |Sodium 518mg | Carbs 7g | Fiber 1.5g | Sugar 3.4g | Protein 12g

Sausage & Butternut Squash

Servings: 2 | Cooking Time: 20 Minutes

Ingredients:

- 450g butternut squash, diced
- 70g kielbasa, diced
- ¼ onion, diced
- ¼ tsp garlic powder
- ½ tbsp olive oil
- Pepper
- Salt

Directions:

1. In a bowl, toss butternut squash with garlic pow-

der, oil, onion, kielbasa, pepper, and salt.
2. Insert a crisper plate in the Ninja Foodi air fryer baskets.
3. Add sausage and butternut squash mixture in both baskets.
4. Select zone 1, then select "air fry" mode and set the temperature to 375 degrees F for 20 minutes. Press "match" to match zone 2 settings to zone 1. Press "start/stop" to begin. Stir halfway through.

Nutrition Info:

• (Per serving) Calories 68 | Fat 3.6g |Sodium 81mg | Carbs 9.7g | Fiber 1.7g | Sugar 2.2g | Protein 0.9g

Roasted Oranges

Servings: 4 | Cooking Time: 6 Minutes

Ingredients:

- 2 oranges, halved
- 2 teaspoons honey
- 1 teaspoon cinnamon

Directions:

1. Place the oranges in each air fryer basket.
2. Drizzle honey and cinnamon over the orange halves.
3. Return the air fryer basket 1 to Zone 1, and basket 2 to Zone 2 of the Ninja Foodi 2-Basket Air Fryer.
4. Choose the "Air Fry" mode for Zone 1 at 395 degrees F temperature and 6 minutes of cooking time.
5. Select the "MATCH COOK" option to copy the settings for Zone 2.
6. Initiate cooking by pressing the START/PAUSE BUTTON.
7. Serve.

Nutrition Info:

• (Per serving) Calories 183 | Fat 15g |Sodium 402mg | Carbs 2.5g | Fiber 0.4g | Sugar 1.1g | Protein 10g

Brussels Sprouts Potato Hash

Servings: 4 | Cooking Time: 10 Minutes

Ingredients:

- 455g Brussels sprouts
- 1 small to medium red onion
- 227g baby red potatoes
- 2 tablespoons avocado oil
- ½ teaspoon salt
- ½ teaspoon black pepper

Directions:

1. Peel and boil potatoes in salted water for 15 minutes until soft.
2. Drain and allow them to cool down then dice.
3. Shred Brussels sprouts and toss them with potatoes and the rest of the ingredients.
4. Divide this veggies hash mixture in both of the air fryer baskets.
5. Return the air fryer basket 1 to Zone 1, and basket 2 to Zone 2 of the Ninja Foodi 2-Basket Air Fryer.
6. Choose the "Air Fry" mode for Zone 1 with 375 degrees F temperature and 10 minutes of cooking time.
7. Select the "MATCH COOK" option to copy the settings for Zone 2.
8. Initiate cooking by pressing the START/PAUSE BUTTON.
9. Shake the veggies once cooked halfway through.
10. Serve warm.

Nutrition Info:

• (Per serving) Calories 305 | Fat 25g |Sodium 532mg | Carbs 2.3g | Fiber 0.4g | Sugar 2g | Protein 18.3g

Biscuit Balls

Servings: 6 | Cooking Time: 18 Minutes.

Ingredients:

- 1 tablespoon butter
- 2 eggs, beaten
- ¼ teaspoon pepper
- 1 can (10.2-oz) Pillsbury Buttermilk biscuits
- 2 ounces cheddar cheese, diced into ten cubes
- Cooking spray
- Egg Wash
- 1 egg
- 1 tablespoon water

Directions:

1. Place a suitable non-stick skillet over medium-high heat and cook the bacon until crispy, then place it on a plate lined with a paper towel.
2. Melt butter in the same skillet over medium heat. Beat eggs with pepper in a bowl and pour them into the skillet.
3. Stir cook for 5 minutes, then remove it from the heat.
4. Add bacon and mix well.
5. Divide the dough into 5 biscuits and slice each into 2 layers.
6. Press each biscuit into 4-inch round.
7. Add a tablespoon of the egg mixture at the center of each round and top it with a piece of cheese.
8. Carefully fold the biscuit dough around the filling and pinch the edges to seal.
9. Whisk egg with water in a small bowl and brush the egg wash over the biscuits.
10. Place half of the biscuit bombs in each of the crisper plate and spray them with cooking oil.
11. Return the crisper plate to the Ninja Foodi Dual Zone Air Fryer.
12. Choose the Air Fry mode for Zone 1 and set the temperature to 375 degrees F and the time to 14 min-

utes.

13. Select the "MATCH" button to copy the settings for Zone 2.

14. Initiate cooking by pressing the START/STOP button.

15. Flip the egg bombs when cooked halfway through, then resume cooking.

16. Serve warm.

Nutrition Info:

- (Per serving) Calories 102 | Fat 7.6g |Sodium 545mg | Carbs 1.5g | Fiber 0.4g | Sugar 0.7g | Protein 7.1g

Glazed Apple Fritters Glazed Peach Fritters

Servings:4 | Cooking Time: 12 Minutes

Ingredients:

- FOR THE FRITTERS
- ¾ cup all-purpose flour
- 2 tablespoons granulated sugar
- 1 teaspoon baking powder
- ½ teaspoon kosher salt
- ½ teaspoon ground cinnamon
- ⅓ cup whole milk
- 2 tablespoons cold unsalted butter, grated
- 1 large egg
- 1 teaspoon fresh lemon juice
- 1 apple, peeled and diced
- 1 peach, peeled and diced
- FOR THE GLAZE
- ½ cup powdered sugar
- 1 tablespoon whole milk
- ½ teaspoon vanilla extract
- ½ teaspoon ground cinnamon
- Pinch salt

Directions:

1. To prep the fritters: In a large bowl, combine the flour, granulated sugar, baking powder, salt, and cinnamon. Stir in the milk, butter, egg, and lemon juice to form a thick batter.
2. Transfer half of the batter to a second bowl. Fold the apples into one bowl and the peaches into the other.
3. To prep the glaze: In a small bowl, whisk together the powdered sugar, milk, vanilla, cinnamon, and salt until smooth. Set aside.
4. To cook the fritters: Install a crisper plate in each of the two baskets. Drop two ¼-cup scoops of the apple fritter batter into the Zone 1 basket and insert the basket in the unit. Drop two ¼-cup scoops of the peach fritter batter into the Zone 2 basket and insert the basket in the unit.
5. Select Zone 1, select AIR FRY, set the temperature to 345°F, and set the time to 10 minutes.
6. Select Zone 2, select AIR FRY, set the temperature to 345°F, and set the time to 12 minutes. Select SMART FINISH.
7. Press START/PAUSE to begin cooking.
8. When cooking is complete, transfer the fritters to a wire rack and drizzle the glaze over them. Serve warm or at room temperature.

Nutrition Info:

- (Per serving) Calories: 298; Total fat: 8g; Saturated fat: 4.5g; Carbohydrates: 53g; Fiber: 3g; Protein: 5g; Sodium: 170mg

Cinnamon Apple French Toast

Servings: 8 | Cooking Time: 10 Minutes

Ingredients:

- 1 egg, lightly beaten
- 4 bread slices
- 1 tbsp cinnamon
- 15ml milk
- 23ml maple syrup
- 45 ml applesauce

Directions:

1. In a bowl, whisk egg, milk, cinnamon, applesauce, and maple syrup.
2. Insert a crisper plate in the Ninja Foodi air fryer baskets.
3. Dip each slice in egg mixture and place in both baskets.
4. Select zone 1 then select "air fry" mode and set the temperature to 355 degrees F for 10 minutes. Press "match" to match zone 2 settings to zone 1. Press "start/stop" to begin.

Nutrition Info:

- (Per serving) Calories 64 | Fat 1.5g |Sodium 79mg | Carbs 10.8g | Fiber 1.3g | Sugar 4.8g | Protein 2.3g

Sausage With Eggs

Servings:2 | Cooking Time:13

Ingredients:

- 4 sausage links, raw and uncooked
- 4 eggs, uncooked
- 1 tablespoon of green onion
- 2 tablespoons of chopped tomatoes
- Salt and black pepper, to taste
- 2 tablespoons of milk, dairy
- Oil spray, for greasing

Directions:

1. Take a bowl and whisk eggs in it.
2. Then pour milk, and add onions and tomatoes.

3. Whisk it all well.
4. Now season it with salt and black pepper.
5. Take one cake pan, that fit inside the air fryer and grease it with oil spray.
6. Pour the omelet in the greased cake pans.
7. Put the cake pan inside zone 1 air fryer basket of Ninja Foodie 2-Basket Air Fryer.
8. Now place the sausage link into the zone 2 basket.
9. Select bake for zone 1 basket and set the timer to 8-10 minutes at 300 degrees F.
10. For the zone 2 basket, select the AIR FRY button and set the timer to 12 minutes at 390 degrees.
11. Once the cooking cycle completes, serve by transferring it to plates.
12. Chop the sausage or cut it in round and then mix it with omelet.
13. Enjoy hot as a delicious breakfast.

Nutrition Info:

- (Per serving) Calories 240 | Fat 18.4g| Sodium 396mg | Carbs 2.8g | Fibero.2g | Sugar 2g | Protein 15.6g

Quiche Breakfast Peppers

Servings: 4 | Cooking Time: 15 Minutes

Ingredients:

- 4 eggs
- ½ tsp garlic powder
- 112g mozzarella cheese, shredded
- 125g ricotta cheese
- 2 bell peppers, cut in half & remove seeds
- 7½g baby spinach, chopped
- 22g parmesan cheese, grated
- ¼ tsp dried parsley

Directions:

1. In a bowl, whisk eggs, ricotta cheese, garlic powder, parsley, cheese, and spinach.
2. Pour the egg mixture into each bell pepper half and top with mozzarella cheese.
3. Insert a crisper plate in the Ninja Foodi air fryer baskets.
4. Place bell peppers in both the baskets.
5. Select zone 1 then select "air fry" mode and set the temperature to 355 degrees F for 15 minutes. Press "match" to match zone 2 settings to zone 1. Press "start/stop" to begin.

Nutrition Info:

- (Per serving) Calories 136 | Fat 7.6g |Sodium 125mg | Carbs 6.9g | Fiber 0.9g | Sugar 3.5g | Protein 10.8g

Sausage Hash And Baked Eggs

Servings:4 | Cooking Time: 30 Minutes

Ingredients:

- FOR THE HASH
- 2 yellow potatoes (about 1 pound), cut into ½-inch pieces
- 4 garlic cloves, minced
- 1 teaspoon kosher salt
- ¼ teaspoon freshly ground black pepper
- 2 tablespoons olive oil
- ½ pound pork breakfast sausage meat
- 1 small yellow onion, diced
- 1 red bell pepper, diced
- 1 teaspoon Italian seasoning
- FOR THE EGGS
- Nonstick cooking spray
- 4 large eggs
- 4 tablespoons water

Directions:

1. To prep the hash: In a large bowl, combine the potatoes, garlic, salt, black pepper, and olive oil and toss to coat. Crumble in the sausage and mix until combined.
2. To prep the eggs: Mist 4 silicone muffin cups with cooking spray. Crack 1 egg into each muffin cup. Top each egg with 1 tablespoon of water.
3. To cook the hash and eggs: Install a crisper plate in the Zone 1 basket. Place the sausage and potato mixture in the Zone 1 basket and insert the basket in the unit. Place the egg cups in the Zone 2 basket and insert the basket in the unit.
4. Select Zone 1, select AIR FRY, set the temperature to 400°F, and set the time to 30 minutes.
5. Select Zone 2, select BAKE, set the temperature to 325°F, and set the time to 12 minutes. Select SMART FINISH.
6. Press START/PAUSE to begin cooking.
7. When the Zone 1 timer reads 20 minutes, press START/PAUSE. Remove the basket and add the onion, bell pepper, and Italian seasoning to the hash. Mix until combined, breaking up any large pieces of sausage. Reinsert the basket and press START/PAUSE to resume cooking.
8. When cooking is complete, serve the hash topped with an egg.

Nutrition Info:

- (Per serving) Calories: 400; Total fat: 23g; Saturated fat: 5.5g; Carbohydrates: 31g; Fiber: 2g; Protein: 19g; Sodium: 750mg

SNACKS AND APPETIZERS RECIPES

Snacks And Appetizers Recipes

Fried Pickles

Servings: 4 | Cooking Time: 15 Minutes

Ingredients:

- 2 cups sliced dill pickles
- 1 cup flour
- 1 tablespoon garlic powder
- 1 tablespoon Cajun spice
- ½ tablespoon cayenne pepper
- Olive Oil or cooking spray

Directions:

1. Mix together the flour and spices in a bowl.
2. Coat the sliced pickles with the flour mixture.
3. Place a crisper plate in each drawer. Put the pickles in a single layer in each drawer. Insert the drawers into the unit.
4. Select zone 1, then AIR FRY, then set the temperature to 400 degrees F/ 200 degrees C with a 15-minute timer. To match zone 2 settings to zone 1, choose MATCH. To begin, select START/STOP.

Nutrition Info:

- (Per serving) Calories 161 | Fat 4.1g | Sodium 975mg | Carbs 27.5g | Fiber 2.2g | Sugar 1.5g | Protein 4g

Jalapeño Popper Chicken

Servings: 4 | Cooking Time: 50 Minutes

Ingredients:

- 2 ounces cream cheese, softened
- ¼ cup shredded cheddar cheese
- ¼ cup shredded mozzarella cheese
- ¼ teaspoon garlic powder
- 4 small jalapeño peppers, seeds removed and diced
- Kosher salt, as desired
- Ground black pepper, as desired
- 4 organic boneless, skinless chicken breasts
- 8 slices bacon

Directions:

1. Cream together the cream cheese, cheddar cheese, mozzarella cheese, garlic powder, and jalapeño in a mixing bowl. Add salt and pepper to taste.
2. Make a deep pocket in the center of each chicken breast, but be cautious not to cut all the way through.
3. Fill each chicken breast's pocket with the cream cheese mixture.
4. Wrap two strips of bacon around each chicken breast and attach them with toothpicks.
5. Place a crisper plate in each drawer. Put the chicken breasts in the drawers. Place both drawers in the unit.
6. Select zone 1, then AIR FRY, and set the temperature to 350 degrees F/ 175 degrees C with a 30-minute timer. To match zone 2 and zone 1 settings, select MATCH. To begin cooking, press the START/STOP button.
7. When cooking is complete, remove the chicken breasts and allow them to rest for 5 minutes before serving

Nutrition Info:

- (Per serving) Calories 507 | Fat 27.5g | Sodium 1432mg | Carbs 2.3g | Fiber 0.6g | Sugar 0.6g | Protein 58.2g

Ravioli

Servings: 2 | Cooking Time: 6 Minutes

Ingredients:

- 12 frozen portions of ravioli
- ½ cup buttermilk
- ½ cup Italian breadcrumbs

Directions:

1. Place two bowls side by side. Put the buttermilk in one and breadcrumbs in the other.
2. Dip each piece of ravioli into the buttermilk then breadcrumbs, making sure to coat them as best as possible.
3. Place a crisper plate in both drawers. In each drawer, put four breaded ravioli pieces in a single layer. Insert the drawers into the unit.
4. Select zone 1, then AIR FRY, then set the temperature to 360 degrees F/ 180 degrees C with a 6-minute timer. To match zone 2 settings to zone 1, choose MATCH. To begin, select START/STOP.
5. Remove the ravioli from the drawers after the timer has finished.

Nutrition Info:

- (Per serving) Calories 481 | Fat 20g | Sodium 1162mg | Carbs 56g | Fiber 4g | Sugar 9g | Protein 19g

Buffalo Wings Honey-garlic Wings

Servings:6 | Cooking Time: 40 Minutes

Ingredients:

- FOR THE BUFFALO WINGS
- 2 pounds chicken wings
- ¼ teaspoon kosher salt
- ¼ teaspoon freshly ground black pepper
- ¼ teaspoon paprika
- 1 tablespoon vegetable oil
- ⅓ cup Buffalo wing sauce
- FOR THE HONEY-GARLIC WINGS
- 2 pounds chicken wings
- 2 tablespoons all-purpose flour
- ½ teaspoon garlic powder
- 1 tablespoon vegetable oil
- ¼ cup honey
- 2 tablespoons reduced-sodium soy sauce
- ½ teaspoon ground ginger (optional)

Directions:

1. To prep the Buffalo wings: In a large bowl, combine the wings, salt, black pepper, and paprika and toss to coat the wings with the seasonings. Drizzle with the oil.
2. To prep the honey-garlic wings: In another large bowl, combine the wings, flour, and garlic powder and toss to coat the wings. Drizzle with the oil.
3. In a small bowl, whisk together the honey, soy sauce, and ginger (if using). Set the honey-soy sauce aside.
4. To cook the wings: Install a crisper plate in each of the two baskets. Place the Buffalo wings in the Zone 1 basket and insert the basket in the unit. Place the honey-garlic wings in the Zone 2 basket and insert the basket in the unit.
5. Select Zone 1, select AIR FRY, set the temperature to 390°F, and set the time to 40 minutes. Select MATCH COOK to match Zone 2 settings to Zone 1.
6. Press START/PAUSE to begin cooking.
7. When both timers read 8 minutes, press START/PAUSE. Remove the Zone 1 basket, drizzle the Buffalo sauce over the wings, and shake to coat the wings with the sauce. Reinsert the basket. Remove the Zone 2 basket, drizzle the honey-soy sauce over the wings, and shake to coat the wings with the sauce. Reinsert the basket. Press START/PAUSE to resume cooking.
8. When cooking is complete, the wings will be golden brown and cooked through. Use silicone-tipped tongs to transfer the wings to a serving plate. Serve warm.

Nutrition Info:

- (Per serving) Calories: 399; Total fat: 28g; Saturated fat: 7.5g; Carbohydrates: 0g; Fiber: 0g; Protein: 34g; Sodium: 1,049mg

Cheddar Quiche

Servings:2 | Cooking Time:12

Ingredients:

- 4 eggs, organic
- 1-1/4 cup heavy cream
- Salt, pinch
- ½ cup broccoli florets
- ½ cup cheddar cheese, shredded and for sprinkling

Directions:

1. Take a Pyrex pitcher and crack two eggs in it.
2. And fill it with heavy cream, about half the way up.
3. Add in the salt and then add in the broccoli and pour this into two quiche dishes, and top it with shredded cheddar cheese.
4. Now divide it between both zones of baskets.
5. For zone 1, set the time to 10-12 minutes at 325 degrees F.
6. Select the MATCH button for the zone 2 basket.
7. Once done, serve hot.

Nutrition Info:

- (Per serving) Calories 454| Fat40g | Sodium 406mg | Carbs 4.2g | Fiber 0.6g| Sugar1.3 g | Protein 20g

Dried Apple Chips Dried Banana Chips

Servings:6 | Cooking Time: 6 To 10 Hours

Ingredients:

- FOR THE APPLE CHIPS
- ½ teaspoon ground cinnamon
- ¼ teaspoon ground nutmeg
- ⅛ teaspoon ground allspice
- ⅛ teaspoon ground ginger
- 2 Gala apples, cored and cut into ⅛-inch-thick rings
- FOR THE BANANA CHIPS
- 2 firm-ripe bananas, cut into ¼-inch slices

Directions:

1. To prep the apple chips: In a small bowl, mix the cinnamon, nutmeg, allspice, and ginger until combined. Sprinkle the spice mixture over the apple slices.
2. To dehydrate the fruit: Arrange half of the apple slices in a single layer in the Zone 1 basket. It is okay if the edges overlap a bit as they will shrink as they cook. Place a crisper plate on top of the apples. Ar-

range the remaining apple slices on top of the crisper plate and insert the basket in the unit.

3. Repeat this process with the bananas in the Zone 2 basket and insert the basket in the unit.

4. Select Zone 1, select DEHYDRATE, set the temperature to 135°F, and set the time to 8 hours.

5. Select Zone 2, select DEHYDRATE, set the temperature to 135°F, and set the time to 10 hours. Select SMART FINISH.

6. Press START/PAUSE to begin cooking.

7. When both timers read 2 hours, press START/PAUSE. Remove both baskets and check the fruit for doneness; note that juicier fruit will take longer to dry than fruit that starts out drier. Reinsert the basket and press START/PAUSE to continue cooking if necessary.

Nutrition Info:

- (Per serving) Calories: 67; Total fat: 0g; Saturated fat: 0g; Carbohydrates: 16g; Fiber: 3g; Protein: 0g; Sodium: 1mg

Zucchini Chips

Servings: 4 | Cooking Time: 15 Minutes

Ingredients:

- 1 medium-sized zucchini
- ½ cup panko breadcrumbs
- ½ teaspoon garlic powder
- ¼ teaspoon onion powder
- 1 egg
- 3 tablespoons flour

Directions:

1. Slice the zucchini into thin slices, about ¼-inch thick.

2. In a mixing bowl, combine the panko breadcrumbs, garlic powder, and onion powder.

3. The egg should be whisked in a different bowl, while the flour should be placed in a third bowl.

4. Dip the zucchini slices in the flour, then in the egg, and finally in the breadcrumbs.

5. Place a crisper plate in each drawer. Put the zucchini slices into each drawer in a single layer. Insert the drawers into the unit.

6. Select zone 1, then AIR FRY, then set the temperature to 360 degrees F/ 180 degrees C with a 6-minute timer. To match zone 2 settings to zone 1, choose MATCH. To begin, select START/STOP.

7. Remove the zucchini from the drawers after the timer has finished.

Nutrition Info:

- (Per serving) Calories 82 | Fat 1.5g | Sodium 89mg | Carbs 14.1g | Fiber 1.7g | Sugar 1.2g | Protein 3.9g

Sweet Bites

Servings:4 | Cooking Time:12

Ingredients:

- 10 sheets of Phyllo dough, (filo dough)
- 2 tablespoons of melted butter
- 1 cup walnuts, chopped
- 2 teaspoons of honey
- Pinch of cinnamon
- 1 teaspoon of orange zest

Directions:

1. First, layer together 10 Phyllo dough sheets on a flat surface.

2. Then cut it into 4 *4-inch squares.

3. Now, coat the squares with butter, drizzle some honey, orange zest, walnuts, and cinnamon.

4. Bring all 4 corners together and press the corners to make a little like purse design.

5. Divide it amongst air fryer basket and select zone 1 basket using AIR fry mode and set it for 7 minutes at 375 degrees F.

6. Select the MATCH button for the zone 2 basket.

7. Once done, take out and serve.

Nutrition Info:

- (Per serving) Calories 397| Fat 27.1 g| Sodium 271mg | Carbs31.2 g | Fiber 3.2g| Sugar3.3g | Protein 11g

Potato Tater Tots

Servings: 4 | Cooking Time: 27 Minutes.

Ingredients:

- 2 potatoes, peeled
- ½ teaspoon Cajun seasoning
- Olive oil cooking spray
- Sea salt to taste

Directions:

1. Boil water in a cooking pot and cook potatoes in it for 15 minutes.

2. Drain and leave the potatoes to cool in a bowl.

3. Grate these potatoes and toss them with Cajun seasoning.

4. Make small tater tots out of this mixture.

5. Divide them into the two crisper plates and spray them with cooking oil.

6. Return the crisper plates to the Ninja Foodi Dual Zone Air Fryer.

7. Choose the Air Fry mode for Zone 1 and set the temperature to 375 degrees F and the time to 27 minutes.

8. Select the "MATCH" button to copy the settings

for Zone 2.
9. Initiate cooking by pressing the START/STOP button.
10. Flip them once cooked halfway through, and resume cooking.
11. Serve warm

Nutrition Info:

- (Per serving) Calories 185 | Fat 11g |Sodium 355mg | Carbs 21g | Fiber 5.8g | Sugar 3g | Protein 4.7g

Mozzarella Balls

Servings: 6 | Cooking Time: 13 Minutes

Ingredients:

- 2 cups mozzarella, shredded
- 3 tablespoons cornstarch
- 3 tablespoons water
- 2 eggs, beaten
- 1 cup Italian seasoned breadcrumbs
- 1 tablespoon Italian seasoning
- 1½ teaspoons garlic powder
- 1 teaspoon salt
- 1½ teaspoons Parmesan

Directions:

1. Mix mozzarella with parmesan, water and cornstarch in a bowl.
2. Make 1-inch balls out of this mixture.
3. Mix breadcrumbs with seasoning, salt, and garlic powder in a bowl.
4. Dip the balls into the beaten eggs and coat with the breadcrumbs.
5. Place the coated balls in the air fryer baskets.
6. Return the air fryer basket 1 to Zone 1, and basket 2 to Zone 2 of the Ninja Foodi 2-Basket Air Fryer.
7. Choose the "Air Fry" mode for Zone 1 and set the temperature to 360 degrees F and 13 minutes of cooking time.
8. Select the "MATCH COOK" option to copy the settings for Zone 2.
9. Initiate cooking by pressing the START/PAUSE BUTTON.
10. Toss the balls once cooked halfway through.
11. Serve.

Nutrition Info:

- (Per serving) Calories 307 | Fat 8.6g |Sodium 510mg | Carbs 22.2g | Fiber 1.4g | Sugar 13g | Protein 33.6g

Potato Chips

Servings: 4 | Cooking Time: 16 Minutes

Ingredients:

- 2 large potatoes, peeled and sliced
- 1½ teaspoons salt
- 1½ teaspoons black pepper
- Oil for misting

Directions:

1. Soak potatoes in cold water for 30 minutes then drain.
2. Pat dry the potato slices and toss them with cracked pepper, salt and oil mist.
3. Spread the potatoes in the air fryer basket.
4. Return the air fryer basket 1 to Zone 1, and basket 2 to Zone 2 of the Ninja Foodi 2-Basket Air Fryer.
5. Choose the "Air Fry" mode for Zone 1 at 300 degrees F and 16 minutes of cooking time.
6. Select the "MATCH COOK" option to copy the settings for Zone 2.
7. Initiate cooking by pressing the START/PAUSE BUTTON.
8. Toss the fries once cooked halfway through.
9. Serve warm.

Nutrition Info:

- (Per serving) Calories 122 | Fat 1.8g |Sodium 794mg | Carbs 17g | Fiber 8.9g | Sugar 1.6g | Protein 14.9g

Avocado Fries With Sriracha Dip

Servings: 4 | Cooking Time: 6 Minutes

Ingredients:

- Avocado Fries
- 4 avocados, peeled and cut into sticks
- ¾ cup panko breadcrumbs
- ¼ cup flour
- 2 eggs, beaten
- ½ teaspoon garlic powder
- ½ teaspoon salt
- SRIRACHA-RANCH SAUCE
- ¼ cup ranch dressing
- 1 teaspoon sriracha sauce

Directions:

1. Mix flour with garlic powder and salt in a bowl.
2. Dredge the avocado sticks through the flour mixture.
3. Dip them in the eggs and coat them with breadcrumbs.
4. Place the coated fries in the air fryer baskets.
5. Return the air fryer basket 1 to Zone 1, and basket 2 to Zone 2 of the Ninja Foodi 2-Basket Air Fryer.
6. Choose the "Air Fry" mode for Zone 1 at 400 de-

grees F and 6 minutes of cooking time.
7. Select the "MATCH COOK" option to copy the settings for Zone 2.
8. Initiate cooking by pressing the START/PAUSE BUTTON.
9. Flip the fries once cooked halfway through.
10. Mix all the dipping sauce ingredients in a bowl.
11. Serve the fries with dipping sauce.

Nutrition Info:

- (Per serving) Calories 229 | Fat 1.9 |Sodium 567mg | Carbs 1.9g | Fiber 0.4g | Sugar 0.6g | Protein 11.8g

Onion Rings

Servings: 4 | Cooking Time: 7 Minutes

Ingredients:

- 170g onion, sliced into rings
- ½ cup breadcrumbs
- 2 eggs, beaten
- ½ cup flour
- Salt and black pepper to taste

Directions:

1. Mix flour, black pepper and salt in a bowl.
2. Dredge the onion rings through the flour mixture.
3. Dip them in the eggs and coat with the breadcrumbs.
4. Place the coated onion rings in the air fryer baskets.
5. Return the air fryer basket 1 to Zone 1, and basket 2 to Zone 2 of the Ninja Foodi 2-Basket Air Fryer.
6. Choose the "Air Fry" mode for Zone 1 at 350 degrees F and 7 minutes of cooking time.
7. Select the "MATCH COOK" option to copy the settings for Zone 2.
8. Initiate cooking by pressing the START/PAUSE BUTTON.
9. Shake the rings once cooked halfway through.
10. Serve warm.

Nutrition Info:

- (Per serving) Calories 185 | Fat 11g |Sodium 355mg | Carbs 21g | Fiber 5.8g | Sugar 3g | Protein 4.7g

Healthy Spinach Balls

Servings: 4 | Cooking Time: 10 Minutes

Ingredients:

- 1 egg
- 29g breadcrumbs
- ½ medium onion, chopped
- 225g spinach, blanched & chopped
- 1 carrot, peel & grated
- 1 tbsp cornflour
- 1 tbsp nutritional yeast
- 1 tsp garlic, minced
- ½ tsp garlic powder
- Pepper
- Salt

Directions:

1. Add spinach and remaining ingredients into the mixing bowl and mix until well combined.
2. Insert a crisper plate in the Ninja Foodi air fryer baskets.
3. Make small balls from the spinach mixture and place them in both baskets.
4. Select zone 1, then select "air fry" mode and set the temperature to 390 degrees F for 10 minutes. Press "match" to match zone 2 settings to zone 1. Press "start/stop" to begin.

Nutrition Info:

- (Per serving) Calories 74 | Fat 1.7g |Sodium 122mg | Carbs 11.1g | Fiber 1.9g | Sugar 2g | Protein 4.2g

Tasty Sweet Potato Wedges

Servings: 4 | Cooking Time: 20 Minutes

Ingredients:

- 2 sweet potatoes, peel & cut into wedges
- 1 tbsp BBQ spice rub
- ½ tsp sweet paprika
- 1 tbsp olive oil
- Pepper
- Salt

Directions:

1. In a bowl, toss sweet potato wedges with sweet paprika, oil, BBQ spice rub, pepper, and salt.
2. Insert a crisper plate in the Ninja Foodi air fryer baskets.
3. Add sweet potato wedges in both baskets.
4. Select zone 1 then select "air fry" mode and set the temperature to 390 degrees F for 20 minutes. Press "match" to match zone 2 settings to zone 1. Press "start/stop" to begin. Turn halfway through.

Nutrition Info:

- (Per serving) Calories 87 | Fat 3.6g |Sodium 75mg | Carbs 13.2g | Fiber 2.1g | Sugar 2.8g | Protein 1.1g

Chili-lime Crispy Chickpeas Pizza-seasoned Crispy Chickpeas

Servings:6 | Cooking Time: 20 Minutes

Ingredients:

- FOR THE CHILI-LIME CHICKPEAS
- 1½ cups canned chickpeas, rinsed and drained
- ¼ cup fresh lime juice
- 1 tablespoon olive oil
- 1½ teaspoons chili powder
- ½ teaspoon kosher salt
- FOR THE PIZZA-SEASONED CHICKPEAS
- 1½ cups canned chickpeas, rinsed and drained
- 1 tablespoon olive oil
- 1 tablespoon grated Parmesan cheese
- ½ teaspoon dried basil
- ½ teaspoon dried oregano
- ½ teaspoon kosher salt
- ¼ teaspoon onion powder
- ¼ teaspoon garlic powder
- ¼ teaspoon fennel seeds
- ¼ teaspoon dried thyme
- ¼ teaspoon red pepper flakes (optional)

Directions:

1. To prep the chili-lime chickpeas: In a small bowl, mix the chickpeas, lime juice, olive oil, chili powder, and salt until the chickpeas are well coated.
2. To prep the pizza-seasoned chickpeas: In a small bowl, mix the chickpeas, olive oil, Parmesan, basil, oregano, salt, onion powder, garlic powder, fennel, thyme, and red pepper flakes (if using) until the chickpeas are well coated.
3. To cook the chickpeas: Install a crisper plate in each of the two baskets. Place the chili-lime chickpeas in the Zone 1 basket and insert the basket in the unit. Place the pizza-seasoned chickpeas in the Zone 2 basket and insert the basket in the unit.
4. Select Zone 1, select AIR FRY, set the temperature to 375°F, and set the time to 20 minutes. Select MATCH COOK to match Zone 2 settings to Zone 1.
5. Press START/PAUSE to begin cooking.
6. When both timers read 10 minutes, press START/PAUSE. Remove both baskets and give each basket a shake to redistribute the chickpeas. Reinsert both baskets and press START/PAUSE to resume cooking.
7. When both timers read 5 minutes, press START/PAUSE. Remove both baskets and give each basket a good shake again. Reinsert both baskets and press START/PAUSE to resume cooking.
8. When cooking is complete, the chickpeas will be crisp and golden brown. Serve warm or at room temperature.

Nutrition Info:

- (Per serving) Calories: 145; Total fat: 6.5g; Saturated fat: 0.5g; Carbohydrates: 17g; Fiber: 4.5g; Protein: 5g; Sodium: 348mg

Healthy Chickpea Fritters

Servings: 6 | Cooking Time: 5 Minutes

Ingredients:

- 1 egg
- 425g can chickpeas, rinsed & drained
- ½ tsp ground ginger
- ½ tsp garlic powder
- 1 tsp ground cumin
- 2 green onions, sliced
- 15g fresh cilantro, chopped
- ½ tsp baking soda
- ½ tsp salt

Directions:

1. Add chickpeas and remaining ingredients into the food processor and process until well combined.
2. Insert a crisper plate in the Ninja Foodi air fryer baskets.
3. Make patties from the mixture and place them in both baskets.
4. Select zone 1, then select "air fry" mode and set the temperature to 390 degrees F for 5 minutes. Press "match" to match zone 2 settings to zone 1. Press "start/stop" to begin.

Nutrition Info:

- (Per serving) Calories 94 | Fat 1.6g |Sodium 508mg | Carbs 15.9g | Fiber 3.2g | Sugar 0.3g | Protein 4.4g

Bacon Wrapped Tater Tots

Servings: 8 | Cooking Time: 14 Minutes

Ingredients:

- 8 bacon slices
- 3 tablespoons honey
- ½ tablespoon chipotle chile powder
- 16 frozen tater tots

Directions:

1. Cut the bacon slices in half and wrap each tater tot with a bacon slice.
2. Brush the bacon with honey and drizzle chipotle chile powder over them.
3. Insert a toothpick to seal the bacon.
4. Place the wrapped tots in the air fryer baskets.
5. Return the air fryer basket 1 to Zone 1, and basket 2 to Zone 2 of the Ninja Foodi 2-Basket Air Fryer.
6. Choose the "Air Fry" mode for Zone 1 at 350 degrees F and 14 minutes of cooking time.
7. Select the "MATCH COOK" option to copy the settings for Zone 2.
8. Initiate cooking by pressing the START/PAUSE

BUTTON.
9. Serve warm.

Nutrition Info:

- (Per serving) Calories 100 | Fat 2g |Sodium 480mg | Carbs 4g | Fiber 2g | Sugar 0g | Protein 18g

Fried Halloumi Cheese

Servings: 6 | Cooking Time: 12 Minutes.

Ingredients:

- 1 block of halloumi cheese, sliced
- 2 teaspoons olive oil

Directions:

1. Divide the halloumi cheese slices in the crisper plate.
2. Drizzle olive oil over the cheese slices.
3. Return the crisper plate to the Ninja Foodi Dual Zone Air Fryer.
4. Choose the Air Fry mode for Zone 1 and set the temperature to 360 degrees F and the time to 12 minutes.
5. Flip the cheese slices once cooked halfway through.
6. Serve.

Nutrition Info:

- (Per serving) Calories 186 | Fat 3g |Sodium 223mg | Carbs 31g | Fiber 8.7g | Sugar 5.5g | Protein 9.7g

Strawberries And Walnuts Muffins

Servings:2 | Cooking Time:15

Ingredients:

- Salt, pinch
- 2 eggs, whisked
- 1/3 cup maple syrup
- 1/3 cup coconut oil
- 4 tablespoons of water
- 1 teaspoon of orange zest
- ¼ teaspoon of vanilla extract
- ½ teaspoon of baking powder
- 1 cup all-purpose flour
- 1 cup strawberries, finely chopped
- 1/3 cup walnuts, chopped and roasted

Directions:

1. Take one cup size of 4 ramekins that are oven safe.
2. Layer it with muffin paper.
3. In a bowl and add egg, maple syrup, oil, water, vanilla extract, and orange zest.
4. Whisk it all very well
5. In a separate bowl, mix flour, baking powder, and salt.
6. Now add dry ingredients slowly to wet ingredients.
7. Now pour this batter into ramekins and top it with strawberries and walnuts.
8. Now divide it between both zones and set the time for zone 1 basket to 15 minutes at 350 degrees F.
9. Select the MATCH button for the zone 2 basket.
10. Check if not done let it AIR FRY FOR one more minute.
11. Once done, serve.

Nutrition Info:

- (Per serving) Calories 897| Fat 53.9g | Sodium 148mg | Carbs 92g | Fiber 4.7g| Sugar35.6 g | Protein 17.5g

Parmesan French Fries

Servings: 6 | Cooking Time: 20 Minutes.

Ingredients:

- 3 medium russet potatoes
- 2 tablespoons parmesan cheese
- 2 tablespoons fresh parsley, chopped
- 1 tablespoon olive oil
- Salt, to taste

Directions:

1. Wash the potatoes and pass them through the fries' cutter to get ¼-inch-thick fries.
2. Place the fries in a colander and drizzle salt on top.
3. Leave these fries for 10 minutes, then rinse.
4. Toss the potatoes with parmesan cheese, oil, salt, and parsley in a bowl.
5. Divide the potatoes into the two crisper plates.
6. Return the crisper plates to the Ninja Foodi Dual Zone Air Fryer.
7. Choose the Air Fry mode for Zone 1 and set the temperature to 360 degrees F and the time to 20 minutes.
8. Select the "MATCH" button to copy the settings for Zone 2.
9. Initiate cooking by pressing the START/STOP button.
10. Toss the chips once cooked halfway through, then resume cooking.
11. Serve warm.

Nutrition Info:

- (Per serving) Calories 307 | Fat 8.6g |Sodium 510mg | Carbs 22.2g | Fiber 1.4g | Sugar 13g | Protein 33.6g

Chicken Tenders

Servings:3 | Cooking Time:12

Ingredients:

- 1 pound of chicken tender
- Salt and black pepper, to taste
- 1 cup Panko bread crumbs
- 2 cups Italian bread crumbs
- 1 cup parmesan cheese
- 2 eggs
- Oil spray, for greasing

Directions:

1. Sprinkle the tenders with salt and black pepper.
2. In a medium bowl mix Panko bread crumbs with Italian breadcrumbs.
3. Add salt, pepper, and parmesan cheese.
4. Crack two eggs in a bowl.
5. First, put the chicken tender in eggs.
6. Now dredge the tender in a bowl and coat the tender well with crumbs.
7. Line both of the baskets of the air fryer with parchment paper.
8. At the end spray the tenders with oil spray.
9. Divided the tenders between the baskets of Ninja Foodie 2-Basket Air Fryer.
10. Set zone 1 basket to AIR FRY mode at 350 degrees F for 12 minutes.
11. Select the MATCH button for the zone 2 basket.
12. Once it's done, serve.

Nutrition Info:

- (Per serving) Calories558 | Fat23.8g | Sodium872 mg | Carbs 20.9g | Fiber1.7 g| Sugar2.2 g | Protein 63.5g

Blueberries Muffins

Servings:2 | Cooking Time:15

Ingredients:

- Salt, pinch
- 2 eggs
- 1/3 cup sugar
- 1/3 cup vegetable oil
- 4 tablespoons of water
- 1 teaspoon of lemon zest
- ¼ teaspoon of vanilla extract
- ½ teaspoon of baking powder
- 1 cup all-purpose flour
- 1 cup blueberries

Directions:

1. Take 4 one-cup sized ramekins that are oven safe and layer them with muffin papers.
2. Take a bowl and whisk the egg, sugar, oil, water, vanilla extract, and lemon zest.
3. Whisk it all very well.
4. Now, in a separate bowl, mix the flour, baking powder, and salt.
5. Now, add dry ingredients slowly to wet ingredients.
6. Now, pour this batter into ramekins and top it with blueberries.
7. Now, divide it between both zones of the Ninja Foodie 2-Basket Air Fryer.
8. Set the time for zone 1 to 15 minutes at 350 degrees F.
9. Select the MATCH button for the zone 2 basket.
10. Check if not done, and let it AIR FRY for one more minute.
11. Once it is done, serve.

Nutrition Info:

- (Per serving) Calories 781| Fat41.6g | Sodium 143mg | Carbs 92.7g | Fiber 3.5g| Sugar41.2 g | Protein 0g

Miso-glazed Shishito Peppers Charred Lemon Shishito Peppers

Servings:4 | Cooking Time: 10 Minutes

Ingredients:

- FOR THE MISO-GLAZED PEPPERS
- 2 tablespoons vegetable oil
- 2 tablespoons water
- 1 tablespoon white miso
- 1 teaspoon grated fresh ginger
- ½ pound shishito peppers
- FOR THE CHARRED LEMON PEPPERS
- ½ pound shishito peppers
- 1 lemon, cut into ⅛-inch-thick rounds
- 2 garlic cloves, minced
- 2 tablespoons vegetable oil
- ½ teaspoon kosher salt

Directions:

1. To prep the miso-glazed peppers: In a large bowl, mix the vegetable oil, water, miso, and ginger until well combined. Add the shishitos and toss to coat.
2. To prep the charred lemon peppers: In a large bowl, combine the shishitos, lemon slices, garlic, vegetable oil, and salt. Toss to coat.
3. To cook the peppers: Install a crisper plate in each of the two baskets. Place the miso-glazed peppers in the Zone 1 basket and insert the basket in the unit. Place the peppers with lemons in the Zone 2 basket and insert the basket in the unit.
4. Select Zone 1, select AIR FRY, set the temperature to 390°F, and set the time to 10 minutes. Select MATCH COOK to match Zone 2 settings to Zone 1.

5. Press START/PAUSE to begin cooking.
6. When both timers read 4 minutes, press START/PAUSE. Remove both baskets and shake well. Reinsert the baskets and press START/PAUSE to resume cooking.
7. When cooking is complete, serve immediately.

Nutrition Info:

- (Per serving) Calories: 165; Total fat: 14g; Saturated fat: 2g; Carbohydrates: 9g; Fiber: 2g; Protein: 2g; Sodium: 334mg

Stuffed Bell Peppers

Servings:3 | Cooking Time:16

Ingredients:

- 6 large bell peppers
- 1-1/2 cup cooked rice
- 2 cups cheddar cheese

Directions:

1. Cut the bell peppers in half lengthwise and remove all the seeds.
2. Fill the cavity of each bell pepper with cooked rice.
3. Divide the bell peppers amongst the two zones of the air fryer basket.
4. Set the time for zone 1 for 200 degrees for 10 minutes.
5. Select MATCH button of zone 2 basket.
6. Afterward, take out the baskets and sprinkle cheese on top.
7. Set the time for zone 1 for 200 degrees for 6 minutes.
8. Select MATCH button of zone 2 basket.
9. Once it's done, serve.

Nutrition Info:

- (Per serving) Calories 605| Fat 26g | Sodium477 mg | Carbs68.3 g | Fiber4 g| Sugar 12.5g | Protein25.6 g

Fried Cheese

Servings: 4 | Cooking Time: 12 Minutes

Ingredients:

- 1 Mozzarella cheese block, cut into sticks
- 2 teaspoons olive oil

Directions:

1. Divide the cheese slices into the Ninja Foodi 2 Baskets Air Fryer baskets.
2. Drizzle olive oil over the cheese slices.
3. Return the air fryer basket 1 to Zone 1, and basket 2 to Zone 2 of the Ninja Foodi 2-Basket Air Fryer.
4. Choose the "Air Fry" mode for Zone 1 and set the temperature to 360 degrees F and 12 minutes of cooking time.
5. Flip the cheese slices once cooked halfway through.
6. Serve.

Nutrition Info:

- (Per serving) Calories 186 | Fat 3g |Sodium 223mg | Carbs 31g | Fiber 8.7g | Sugar 5.5g | Protein 9.7g

FISH AND SEAFOOD RECIPES

Fish And Seafood Recipes

Shrimp With Lemon And Pepper

Servings: 4 | Cooking Time: 8 Minutes

Ingredients:

- 455g raw shrimp, peeled and deveined
- 118ml olive oil
- 2 tablespoons lemon juice
- 1 teaspoon black pepper
- ½ teaspoon salt

Directions:

1. Toss shrimp with black pepper, salt, lemon juice and oil in a bowl.
2. Divide the shrimp into the Ninja Foodi 2 Baskets Air Fryer baskets.
3. Return the air fryer basket 1 to Zone 1, and basket 2 to Zone 2 of the Ninja Foodi 2-Basket Air Fryer.
4. Choose the "Air Fry" mode for Zone 1 at 350 degrees F and 8 minutes of cooking time.
5. Select the "MATCH COOK" option to copy the settings for Zone 2.
6. Initiate cooking by pressing the START/PAUSE BUTTON.
7. Serve warm.

Nutrition Info:

- (Per serving) Calories 257 | Fat 10.4g |Sodium 431mg | Carbs 20g | Fiber 0g | Sugar 1.6g | Protein 21g

Fish Sandwich

Servings: 4 | Cooking Time: 22 Minutes.

Ingredients:

- 4 small cod fillets, skinless
- Salt and black pepper, to taste
- 2 tablespoons flour
- ¼ cup dried breadcrumbs
- Spray oil
- 9 ounces of frozen peas
- 1 tablespoon creme fraiche
- 12 capers
- 1 squeeze of lemon juice
- 4 bread rolls, cut in halve

Directions:

1. First, coat the cod fillets with flour, salt, and black pepper.
2. Then coat the fish with breadcrumbs.
3. Divide the coated codfish in the two crisper plates and spray them with cooking spray.
4. Return the crisper plate to the Ninja Foodi Dual Zone Air Fryer.
5. Choose the Air Fry mode for Zone 1 and set the temperature to 390 degrees F and the time to 17 minutes.
6. Select the "MATCH" button to copy the settings for Zone 2.
7. Initiate cooking by pressing the START/STOP button.
8. Meanwhile, boil peas in hot water for 5 minutes until soft.
9. Then drain the peas and transfer them to the blender.
10. Add capers, lemon juice, and crème fraiche to the blender.
11. Blend until it makes a smooth mixture.
12. Spread the peas crème mixture on top of 2 lower halves of the bread roll, and place the fish fillets on it.
13. Place the remaining bread slices on top.
14. Serve fresh.

Nutrition Info:

- (Per serving) Calories 348 | Fat 30g |Sodium 660mg | Carbs 5g | Fiber 0g | Sugar 0g | Protein 14g

Bang Bang Shrimp With Roasted Bok Choy

Servings:4 | Cooking Time: 13 Minutes

Ingredients:

- FOR THE BANG BANG SHRIMP
- ½ cup all-purpose flour
- 2 large eggs
- 1 cup panko bread crumbs
- 1 pound peeled shrimp (tails removed), thawed if frozen
- Nonstick cooking spray
- ½ cup mayonnaise
- ¼ cup Thai sweet chili sauce
- ¼ teaspoon sriracha
- FOR THE BOK CHOY
- 1 tablespoon reduced-sodium soy sauce
- 1 teaspoon minced garlic
- 1 teaspoon sesame oil
- 1 teaspoon minced fresh ginger
- 1½ pounds baby bok

choy, halved lengthwise
- 1 tablespoon toasted sesame seeds

Directions:

1. To prep the shrimp: Set up a breading station with three small shallow bowls. Place the flour in the first bowl. In the second bowl, whisk the eggs. Place the panko in the third bowl.
2. Bread the shrimp in this order: First, dip them into the flour, coating both sides. Then, dip into the beaten egg. Finally, coat them in the panko, gently pressing the bread crumbs to adhere to the shrimp. Spritz both sides of the shrimp with cooking spray.
3. To prep the bok choy: In a small bowl, whisk together the soy sauce, garlic, sesame oil, and ginger.
4. To cook the shrimp and bok choy: Install a crisper plate in the Zone 1 basket. Place the shrimp in the basket in a single layer and insert the basket in the unit. Place the boy choy cut-side up in the Zone 2 basket. Pour the sauce over the bok choy and insert the basket in the unit.
5. Select Zone 1, select AIR FRY, set the temperature to 390°F, and set the timer to 13 minutes.
6. Select Zone 2, select BAKE, set the temperature to 370°F, and set the timer to 8 minutes. Select SMART FINISH.
7. Press START/PAUSE to begin cooking.
8. When cooking is complete, the shrimp should be cooked through and golden brown and the bok choy soft and slightly caramelized.
9. In a large bowl, whisk together the mayonnaise, sweet chili sauce, and sriracha. Add the shrimp and toss to coat.
10. Sprinkle the bok choy with the sesame seeds and serve hot alongside the shrimp.

Nutrition Info:

- (Per serving) Calories: 534; Total fat: 33g; Saturated fat: 4g; Carbohydrates: 29g; Fiber: 3g; Protein: 31g; Sodium: 789mg

Crispy Fish Nuggets

Servings: 4 | Cooking Time: 8 Minutes

Ingredients:

- 2 eggs
- 96g all-purpose flour
- 700g cod fish fillets, cut into pieces
- 1 tsp garlic powder
- 1 tbsp old bay seasoning
- Pepper
- Salt

Directions:

1. In a small bowl, whisk eggs.
2. Mix flour, garlic powder, old bay seasoning, pepper, and salt in a shallow dish.
3. Coat each fish piece with flour, then dip in egg and again coat with flour.
4. Insert a crisper plate in the Ninja Foodi air fryer baskets.
5. Place coated fish pieces in both baskets.
6. Select zone 1, then select "air fry" mode and set the temperature to 380 degrees F for 8 minutes. Press "match" to match zone 2 settings to zone 1. Press "start/stop" to begin.

Nutrition Info:

- (Per serving) Calories 298 | Fat 3.9g |Sodium 683mg | Carbs 18.6g | Fiber 0.7g | Sugar 0.4g | Protein 44.1g

Chili Lime Tilapia

Servings: 4 | Cooking Time: 10 Minutes

Ingredients:

- 340g tilapia fillets
- 2 teaspoons chili powder
- 1 teaspoon cumin
- 1 teaspoon garlic powder
- ½ teaspoon oregano
- ½ teaspoon sea salt
- ¼ teaspoon black pepper
- Lime zest from 1 lime
- Juice of ½ lime

Directions:

1. Mix chili powder and other spices with lime juice and zest in a bowl.
2. Rub this spice mixture over the tilapia fillets.
3. Place two fillets in each air basket.
4. Return the air fryer basket to the Ninja Foodi 2 Baskets Air Fryer.
5. Choose the "Air Fry" mode for Zone 1 at 400 degrees F and 10 minutes of cooking time.
6. Select the "MATCH COOK" option to copy the settings for Zone 2.
7. Initiate cooking by pressing the START/PAUSE BUTTON.
8. Flip the tilapia fillets once cooked halfway through.
9. Serve warm.

Nutrition Info:

- (Per serving) Calories 275 | Fat 1.4g |Sodium 582mg | Carbs 31.5g | Fiber 1.1g | Sugar 0.1g | Protein 29.8g

Honey Sriracha Mahi Mahi

Servings: 4 | Cooking Time: 7 Minutes

Ingredients:

- 3 pounds mahi-mahi
- 6 tablespoons honey
- 4 tablespoons sriracha
- Salt, to taste
- Cooking spray

Directions:

1. In a small bowl, mix the sriracha sauce and honey. Mix well.
2. Season the fish with salt and pour the honey mixture over it. Let it sit at room temperature for 20 minutes.
3. Place a crisper plate in each drawer. Put the fish in a single layer in each. Insert the drawers into the unit.
4. Select zone 1, then AIR FRY, then set the temperature to 400 degrees F/ 200 degrees C with a 7-minute timer. To match zone 2 settings to zone 1, choose MATCH. To begin, select START/STOP.
5. Remove the fish from the drawers after the timer has finished.

Nutrition Info:

- (Per serving) Calories 581 | Fat 22g | Sodium 495mg | Carbs 26g | Fiber 4g | Sugar 26g | Protein 68g

Pretzel-crusted Catfish

Servings: 4 | Cooking Time: 12 Minutes

Ingredients:

- 4 catfish fillets
- ½ teaspoon salt
- ½ teaspoon black pepper
- 2 large eggs
- ⅓ cup Dijon mustard
- 2 tablespoons 2% milk
- ½ cup all-purpose flour
- 4 cups miniature pretzels, crushed
- Cooking spray
- Lemon slices

Directions:

1. Rub the catfish with black pepper and salt.
2. Beat eggs with milk and mustard in a bowl.
3. Spread pretzels and flour in two separate bowls.
4. Coat the catfish with flour then dip in the egg mixture and coat with the pretzels.
5. Place two fish fillets in each air fryer basket.
6. Return the air fryer basket 1 to Zone 1, and basket 2 to Zone 2 of the Ninja Foodi 2-Basket Air Fryer.
7. Choose the "Air Fry" mode for Zone 1 at 325 degrees F and 12 minutes of cooking time.
8. Select the "MATCH COOK" option to copy the settings for Zone 2.
9. Initiate cooking by pressing the START/PAUSE BUTTON.
10. Serve warm.

Nutrition Info:

- (Per serving) Calories 196 | Fat 7.1g |Sodium 492mg | Carbs 21.6g | Fiber 2.9g | Sugar 0.8g | Protein 13.4g

Herb Lemon Mussels

Servings: 6 | Cooking Time: 10 Minutes

Ingredients:

- 1kg mussels, steamed & half shell
- 1 tbsp thyme, chopped
- 1 tbsp parsley, chopped
- 1 tsp dried parsley
- 1 tsp garlic, minced
- 60ml olive oil
- 45ml lemon juice
- Pepper
- Salt

Directions:

1. In a bowl, mix mussels with the remaining ingredients.
2. Insert a crisper plate in the Ninja Foodi air fryer baskets.
3. Add the mussels to both baskets.
4. Select zone 1 then select "air fry" mode and set the temperature to 360 degrees F for 10 minutes. Press "match" to match zone 2 settings to zone 1. Press "start/stop" to begin.

Nutrition Info:

- (Per serving) Calories 206 | Fat 11.9g |Sodium 462mg | Carbs 6.3g | Fiber 0.3g | Sugar 0.2g | Protein 18.2g

Beer Battered Fish Fillet

Servings:2 | Cooking Time:14

Ingredients:

- 1 cup all-purpose flour
- 4 tablespoons cornstarch
- 1 teaspoon baking soda
- 8 ounces beer
- 2 egg beaten
- ½ cup all-purpose flour
- 1 teaspoon smoked paprika
- 1 teaspoon salt
- 1/4 teaspoon freshly ground black pepper
- ¼ teaspoon of cayenne pepper
- 2 cod fillets, 1½-inches thick, cut into 4 pieces
- Oil spray, for greasing

Directions:

1. Take a large bowl and combine flour, baking soda, corn starch, and salt
2. In a separate bowl beat eggs along with the beer.
3. In a shallow dish mix paprika, salt, pepper, and

cayenne pepper.
4. Dry the codfish fillets with a paper towel.
5. Dip the fish into the eggs and coat it with seasoned flour.
6. Then dip it in the seasoning.
7. Grease the fillet with oil spray.
8. Divide the fillet between both zones.
9. Set zone 1 to AIR FRY mode at 400 degrees F for 14 minutes.
10. Select MACTH button for zone 2 basket.
11. Press start and let the AIR fry do its magic.
12. Once cooking is done, serve the fish.
13. Enjoy it hot.

Nutrition Info:

- (Per serving) Calories 1691| Fat 6.1g| Sodium 3976mg | Carbs105.1 g | Fiber 3.4g | Sugar15.6 g | Protein 270g

Lemon Pepper Salmon With Asparagus

Servings:2 | Cooking Time:18

Ingredients:

- 1 cup of green asparagus
- 2 tablespoons of butter
- 2 fillets of salmon, 8 ounces each
- Salt and black pepper, to taste
- 1 teaspoon of lemon juice
- ½ teaspoon of lemon zest
- oil spray, for greasing

Directions:

1. Rinse and trim the asparagus.
2. Rinse and pat dry the salmon fillets.
3. Take a bowl and mix lemon juice, lemon zest, salt, and black pepper.
4. Brush the fish fillet with the rub and place it in the zone 1 basket.
5. Place asparagus in zone 2 basket.
6. Spray the asparagus with oil spray.
7. Set zone 1 to AIRFRY mode for 18 minutes at 390 degrees F.
8. Set the zone 2 to 5 minutes at 390 degrees F, at air fry mode.
9. Hit the smart finish button to finish at the same time.
10. Once done, serve and enjoy.

Nutrition Info:

- (Per serving) Calories 482| Fat 28g| Sodium209 mg | Carbs 2.8g | Fiber1.5 g | Sugar1.4 g | Protein 56.3g

Fried Tilapia

Servings: 4 | Cooking Time: 20 Minutes

Ingredients:

- 4 fresh tilapia fillets, approximately 6 ounces each
- 2 teaspoons olive oil
- 2 teaspoons chopped fresh chives
- 2 teaspoons chopped fresh parsley
- 1 teaspoon minced garlic
- Freshly ground pepper, to taste
- Salt to taste

Directions:

1. Pat the tilapia fillets dry with a paper towel.
2. Stir together the olive oil, chives, parsley, garlic, salt, and pepper in a small bowl.
3. Brush the mixture over the top of the tilapia fillets.
4. Place a crisper plate in each drawer. Add the fillets in a single layer to each drawer. Insert the drawers into the unit.
5. Select zone 1, then AIR FRY, then set the temperature to 360 degrees F/ 180 degrees C with a 20-minute timer. To match zone 2 settings to zone 1, choose MATCH. To begin, select START/STOP.
6. Remove the tilapia fillets from the drawers after the timer has finished.

Nutrition Info:

- (Per serving) Calories 140 | Fat 5.7g | Sodium 125mg | Carbs 1.5g | Fiber 0.4g | Sugar 0g | Protein 21.7g

Roasted Salmon And Parmesan Asparagus

Servings: 4 | Cooking Time: 27 Minutes

Ingredients:

- 2 tablespoons Montreal steak seasoning
- 3 tablespoons brown sugar
- 3 uncooked salmon fillets (6 ounces each)
- 2 tablespoons canola oil, divided
- 1-pound asparagus, ends trimmed
- Kosher salt, as desired
- Ground black pepper, as desired
- ¼ cup shredded parmesan cheese, divided

Directions:

1. Combine the steak spice and brown sugar in a small bowl.
2. Brush 1 tablespoon of oil over the salmon fillets, then thoroughly coat with the sugar mixture.
3. Toss the asparagus with the remaining 1 tablespoon of oil, salt, and pepper in a mixing bowl.

4. Place a crisper plate in both drawers. Put the fillets skin-side down in the zone 1 drawer, then place the drawer in the unit. Insert the zone 2 drawer into the device after placing the asparagus in it.

5. Select zone 1, then ROAST, then set the temperature to 390 degrees F/ 200 degrees C with a 17-minute timer. To match the zone 2 settings to zone 1, choose MATCH. To begin cooking, press the START/STOP button.

6. When the zone 2 timer reaches 7 minutes, press START/STOP. Remove the zone 2 drawer from the unit. Flip the asparagus with silicone-tipped tongs. Re-insert the drawer into the unit. Continue cooking by pressing START/STOP.

7. When the zone 2 timer has reached 14 minutes, press START/STOP. Remove the zone 2 drawer from the unit. Sprinkle half the parmesan cheese over the asparagus, and mix lightly. Re-insert the drawer into the unit. Continue cooking by pressing START/STOP.

8. Transfer the fillets and asparagus to a serving plate once they've finished cooking. Serve with the remaining parmesan cheese on top of the asparagus.

Nutrition Info:

- (Per serving) Calories 293 | Fat 15.8g | Sodium 203mg | Carbs 11.1g | Fiber 2.4g | Sugar 8.7g | Protein 29g

Savory Salmon Fillets

Servings: 4 | Cooking Time: 17 Minutes.

Ingredients:

- 4 (6-oz) salmon fillets
- Salt, to taste
- Black pepper, to taste
- 4 teaspoons olive oil
- 4 tablespoons wholegrain mustard
- 2 tablespoons packed brown sugar
- 2 garlic cloves, minced
- 1 teaspoon thyme leaves

Directions:

1. Rub the salmon with salt and black pepper first.

2. Whisk oil with sugar, thyme, garlic, and mustard in a small bowl.

3. Place two salmon fillets in each of the crisper plate and brush the thyme mixture on top of each fillet.

4. Return the crisper plates to the Ninja Foodi Dual Zone Air Fryer.

5. Choose the Air Fry mode for Zone 1 and set the temperature to 390 degrees F and the time to 17 minutes.

6. Select the "MATCH" button to copy the settings for Zone 2.

7. Initiate cooking by pressing the START/STOP button.

8. Serve warm and fresh.

Nutrition Info:

- (Per serving) Calories 336 | Fat 6g |Sodium 181mg | Carbs 1.3g | Fiber 0.2g | Sugar 0.4g | Protein 69.2g

"fried" Fish With Seasoned Potato Wedges

Servings:4 | Cooking Time: 30 Minutes

Ingredients:

- FOR THE FISH
- 4 cod fillets (6 ounces each)
- 4 tablespoons all-purpose flour, divided
- ¼ cup cornstarch
- 1 teaspoon baking powder
- ¼ teaspoon kosher salt
- ⅓ cup lager-style beer or sparkling water
- Tartar sauce, cocktail sauce, or malt vinegar, for serving (optional)
- FOR THE POTATOES
- 4 russet potatoes
- 2 tablespoons vegetable oil
- ½ teaspoon paprika
- ½ teaspoon kosher salt
- ¼ teaspoon garlic powder
- ¼ teaspoon freshly ground black pepper

Directions:

1. To prep the fish: Pat the fish dry with a paper towel and coat lightly with 2 tablespoons of flour.

2. In a shallow dish, combine the remaining 2 tablespoons of flour, the cornstarch, baking powder, and salt. Stir in the beer to form a thick batter.

3. Dip the fish in the batter to coat both sides, then let rest on a cutting board for 10 minutes.

4. To prep the potatoes: Cut each potato in half lengthwise, then cut each half into 4 wedges.

5. In a large bowl, combine the potatoes and oil. Toss well to fully coat the potatoes. Add the paprika, salt, garlic powder, and black pepper and toss well to coat.

6. To cook the fish and potato wedges: Install a crisper plate in each of the two baskets. Place a piece of parchment paper or aluminum foil over the plate in the Zone 1 basket. Place the fish in the basket and insert the basket in the unit. Place the potato wedges in a single layer in the Zone 2 basket and insert the basket in the unit.

7. Select Zone 1, select AIR FRY, set the temperature to 400°F, and set the timer to 13 minutes.

8. Select Zone 2, select AIR FRY, set the temperature to 400°F, and set the timer to 30 minutes. Select

SMART FINISH.

9. Press START/PAUSE to begin cooking.

10. When the Zone 1 timer reads 5 minutes, press START/PAUSE. Remove the basket and use a silicone spatula to carefully flip the fish over. Reinsert the basket and press START/PAUSE to resume cooking.

11. When cooking is complete, the fish should be cooked through and the potatoes crispy outside and tender inside. Serve hot with tartar sauce, cocktail sauce, or malt vinegar (if using).

Nutrition Info:

- (Per serving) Calories: 360; Total fat: 8g; Saturated fat: 1g; Carbohydrates: 40g; Fiber: 2g; Protein: 30g; Sodium: 302mg

Smoked Salmon

Servings:4 | Cooking Time:12

Ingredients:

- 2 pounds of salmon fillets, smoked
- 6 ounces cream cheese
- 4 tablespoons mayonnaise
- 2 teaspoons of chives, fresh
- 1 teaspoon of lemon zest
- Salt and freshly ground black pepper, to taste
- 2 tablespoons of butter

Directions:

1. Cut the salmon into very small and uniform bite-size pieces.
2. Mix cream cheese, chives, mayonnaise, black pepper, and lemon zest, in a small mixing bowl.
3. Let it sit aside for further use.
4. Coat the salmon pieces with salt and butter.
5. Divide the bite-size pieces into both zones of the air fryer.
6. Set it on AIRFRY mode at 400 degrees F for 12 minutes.
7. Select MATCH for zone 2 basket.
8. Hit start, so the cooking start.
9. Once the salmon is done, top it with a bowl creamy mixture and serve.
10. Enjoy hot.

Nutrition Info:

- (Per serving) Calories 557| Fat 15.7 g| Sodium 371mg | Carbs 4.8 g | Fiber 0g | Sugar 1.1g | Protein 48 g

Two-way Salmon

Servings:2 | Cooking Time:18

Ingredients:

- 2 salmon fillets, 8 ounces each
- 2 tablespoons of Cajun seasoning
- 2 tablespoons of jerk seasoning
- 1 lemon cut in half
- oil spray, for greasing

Directions:

1. First, drizzle lemon juice over the salmon and wash it with tap water.
2. Rinse and pat dry the fillets with a paper towel.
3. Now rub o fillet with Cajun seasoning and grease it with oil spray.
4. Take the second fillet and rub it with jerk seasoning.
5. Grease the second fillet of salmon with oil spray.
6. now put the salmon fillets in both the baskets.
7. Set the Zone 1 basket to 390 degrees F for 16-18 minutes
8. Select MATCH button for zone 2 basket.
9. hit the start button to start cooking.
10. Once the cooking is done, serve the fish hot with mayonnaise.

Nutrition Info:

- (Per serving) Calories 238| Fat 11.8g| Sodium 488mg | Carbs 9g | Fiber 0g | Sugar8 g | Protein 35g

Lemon Pepper Fish Fillets

Servings: 4 | Cooking Time: 10 Minutes

Ingredients:

- 4 tilapia fillets
- 30ml olive oil
- 2 tbsp lemon zest
- ⅛ tsp paprika
- 1 tsp garlic, minced
- 1 ½ tsp ground peppercorns
- Pepper
- Salt

Directions:

1. In a small bowl, mix oil, peppercorns, paprika, garlic, lemon zest, pepper, and salt.
2. Brush the fish fillets with oil mixture.
3. Insert a crisper plate in the Ninja Foodi air fryer baskets.
4. Place fish fillets in both baskets.
5. Select zone 1 then select "air fry" mode and set the temperature to 390 degrees F for 10 minutes. Press "match" to match zone 2 settings to zone 1. Press "start/stop" to begin.

Nutrition Info:

- (Per serving) Calories 203 | Fat 9g |Sodium 99mg | Carbs 0.9g | Fiber 0.2g | Sugar 0.2g | Protein 32.1g

Scallops With Greens

Servings: 8 | Cooking Time: 13 Minutes.

Ingredients:

- ¾ cup heavy whipping cream
- 1 tablespoon tomato paste
- 1 tablespoon chopped fresh basil
- 1 teaspoon garlic, minced
- ½ teaspoons salt
- ½ teaspoons pepper
- 12 ounces frozen spinach thawed
- 8 jumbo sea scallops
- Vegetable oil to spray

Directions:

1. Season the scallops with vegetable oil, salt, and pepper in a bowl
2. Mix cream with spinach, basil, garlic, salt, pepper, and tomato paste in a bowl.
3. Pour this mixture over the scallops and mix gently.
4. Divide the scallops in the Air Fryers Baskets without using the crisper plate.
5. Return the crisper plate to the Ninja Foodi Dual Zone Air Fryer.
6. Choose the Air Fry mode for Zone 1 and set the temperature to 390 degrees F and the time to 13 minutes.
7. Select the "MATCH" button to copy the settings for Zone 2.
8. Initiate cooking by pressing the START/STOP button.
9. Serve right away

Nutrition Info:

- (Per serving) Calories 266 | Fat 6.3g |Sodium 193mg | Carbs 39.1g | Fiber 7.2g | Sugar 5.2g | Protein 14.8g

Salmon With Broccoli And Cheese

Servings:2 | Cooking Time:18

Ingredients:

- 2 cups of broccoli
- ½ cup of butter, melted
- Salt and pepper, to taste
- Oil spray, for greasing
- 1 cup of grated cheddar cheese
- 1 pound of salmon, fillets

Directions:

1. Take a bowl and add broccoli to it.
2. Add salt and black pepper and spray it with oil.
3. Put the broccoli in the air fryer zone 1 backset.
4. Now rub the salmon fillets with salt, black pepper, and butter.
5. Put it into zone 2 baskets.
6. Set zone 1 to air fry mode for 5 minters at 400 degrees F.
7. Set zone 2 to air fry mode for 18 minutes at 390 degrees F.
8. Hit start to start the cooking.
9. Once done, serve and by placing it on serving plates.
10. Put the grated cheese on top of the salmon and serve.

Nutrition Info:

- (Per serving) Calories 966 | Fat 79.1 g| Sodium 808 mg | Carbs 6.8 g | Fiber 2.4g | Sugar 1.9g | Protein 61.2 g

Parmesan-crusted Fish Sticks With Baked Macaroni And Cheese

Servings:4 | Cooking Time: 25 Minutes

Ingredients:

- FOR THE FISH STICKS
- 1 pound cod or haddock fillets
- ½ cup all-purpose flour
- 2 large eggs
- ¼ teaspoon kosher salt
- ¼ teaspoon freshly ground black pepper
- ¾ cup panko bread crumbs
- ¼ cup grated Parmesan cheese
- Nonstick cooking spray
- FOR THE MACARONI AND CHEESE
- 1½ cups elbow macaroni
- 1 cup whole milk
- ½ cup heavy (whipping) cream
- 8 ounces shredded Colby-Jack cheese
- 4 ounces cream cheese, at room temperature
- 1 teaspoon Dijon mustard
- ½ teaspoon kosher salt
- ½ teaspoon freshly ground black pepper

Directions:

1. To prep the fish sticks: Cut the fish into sticks about 3 inches long and ¾ inch wide.
2. Set up a breading station with three small shallow bowls. Place the flour in the first bowl. In the second bowl, whisk the eggs and season with the salt and black pepper. Combine the panko and Parmesan in the third bowl.
3. Bread the fish sticks in this order: First, dip them into the flour, coating all sides. Then, dip into the beaten egg. Finally, coat them in the panko mixture, gently pressing the bread crumbs into the fish. Spritz

each fish stick all over with cooking spray.

4. To prep the macaroni and cheese: Place the macaroni in the Zone 2 basket. Add the milk, cream, Colby-Jack, cream cheese, mustard, salt, and black pepper. Stir well to combine, ensuring the pasta is completely submerged in the liquid.

5. To cook the fish sticks and macaroni and cheese: Install a crisper plate in the Zone 1 basket. Arrange the fish sticks in a single layer in the basket (use a rack or cook in batches if necessary) and insert the basket in the unit. Insert the Zone 2 basket in the unit.

6. Select Zone 1, select AIR FRY, set the temperature to 390°F, and set the timer to 18 minutes.

7. Select Zone 2, select BAKE, set the temperature to 360°F, and set the timer to 25 minutes. Select SMART FINISH.

8. Press START/PAUSE to begin cooking.

9. When the Zone 1 timer reads 3 minutes, press START/PAUSE. Remove the basket and use silicone-tipped tongs to gently flip over the fish sticks. Reinsert the basket and press START/PAUSE to resume cooking.

10. When cooking is complete, the fish sticks should be crisp and the macaroni tender.

11. Stir the macaroni and cheese and let stand for 5 minutes before serving. The sauce will thicken as it cools.

Nutrition Info:

- (Per serving) Calories: 903; Total fat: 51g; Saturated fat: 25g; Carbohydrates: 60g; Fiber: 2.5g; Protein: 48g; Sodium: 844mg

Spicy Fish Fillet With Onion Rings

Servings:1 | Cooking Time:12

Ingredients:

- 300 grams of onion rings, frozen and packed
- 1 codfish fillet, 8 ounces
- Salt and black pepper, to taste
- 1 teaspoon of lemon juice
- oil spray, for greasing

Directions:

1. Put the frozen onion rings in zone 1 basket of the air fryer.

2. Next pat dry the fish fillets with a paper towel and season them with salt, black pepper, and lemon juice.

3. Grease the fillet with oil spray.

4. Put the fish in zone 2 basket.

5. Use MAX crisp for zone 1 at 240 degrees for 9 minutes.

6. Use MAX crisp for zone 2 basket and set it to 210 degrees for 12 minutes.

7. Press sync and press start.

8. Once done, serve hot.

Nutrition Info:

- (Per serving) Calories 666| Fat23.5g| Sodium 911mg | Carbs 82g | Fiber 8.8g | Sugar 17.4g | Protein 30.4g

Salmon Patties

Servings: 8 | Cooking Time: 18 Minutes.

Ingredients:

- 1 lb. fresh Atlantic salmon side
- ¼ cup avocado, mashed
- ¼ cup cilantro, diced
- 1 ½ teaspoons yellow curry powder
- ½ teaspoons sea salt
- ¼ cup, 4 teaspoons tapioca starch
- 2 brown eggs
- ½ cup coconut flakes
- Coconut oil, melted, for brushing
- For the greens:
- 2 teaspoons organic coconut oil, melted
- 6 cups arugula & spinach mix, tightly packed
- Pinch of sea salt

Directions:

1. Remove the fish skin and dice the flesh.

2. Place in a large bowl. Add cilantro, avocado, salt, and curry powder mix gently.

3. Add tapioca starch and mix well again.

4. Make 8 salmon patties out of this mixture, about a half-inch thick.

5. Place them on a baking sheet lined with wax paper and freeze them for 20 minutes.

6. Place ¼ cup tapioca starch and coconut flakes on a flat plate.

7. Dip the patties in the whisked egg, then coat the frozen patties in the starch and flakes.

8. Place half of the patties in each of the crisper plate and spray them with cooking oil

9. Return the crisper plate to the Ninja Foodi Dual Zone Air Fryer.

10. Choose the Air Fry mode for Zone 1 and set the temperature to 390 degrees F and the time to 17 minutes.

11. Select the "MATCH" button to copy the settings for Zone 2.

12. Initiate cooking by pressing the START/STOP button.

13. Flip the patties once cooked halfway through, then resume cooking.

14. Sauté arugula with spinach in coconut oil in a pan for 30 seconds.

15. Serve the patties with sautéed greens mixture

Nutrition Info:

- (Per serving) Calories 260 | Fat 16g |Sodium 585mg | Carbs 3.1g | Fiber 1.3g | Sugar 0.2g | Protein 25.5g

Fish Tacos

Servings: 5 | Cooking Time: 30 Minutes

Ingredients:

- 1 pound firm white fish such as cod, haddock, pollock, halibut, or walleye
- ¾ cup gluten-free flour blend
- 3 eggs
- 1 cup gluten-free panko breadcrumbs
- 1 teaspoon garlic powder
- 1 teaspoon onion powder
- 1 teaspoon cumin
- 1 teaspoon lemon pepper
- 1 teaspoon red chili flakes
- 1 teaspoon kosher salt, divided
- 1 teaspoon pepper, divided
- Cooking oil spray
- 1 package corn tortillas
- Toppings such as tomatoes, avocado, cabbage, radishes, jalapenos, salsa, or hot sauce (optional)

Directions:

1. Dry the fish with paper towels. (Make sure to thaw the fish if it's frozen.) Depending on the size of the fillets, cut the fish in half or thirds.
2. On both sides of the fish pieces, liberally season with salt and pepper.
3. Put the flour in a dish.
4. In a separate bowl, crack the eggs and whisk them together until well blended.
5. Put the panko breadcrumbs in another bowl. Add the garlic powder, onion powder, cumin, lemon pepper, and red chili flakes. Add salt and pepper to taste. Stir until everything is well blended.
6. Each piece of fish should be dipped in the flour, then the eggs, and finally in the breadcrumb mixture. Make sure that each piece is completely coated.
7. Put a crisper plate in each drawer. Arrange the fish pieces in a single layer in each drawer. Insert the drawers into the unit.
8. Select zone 1, then AIR FRY, then set the temperature to 360 degrees F/ 180 degrees C with a 20-minute timer. To match zone 2 settings to zone 1, choose MATCH. To begin, select START/STOP.
9. Remove the fish from the drawers after the timer has finished. Place the crispy fish on warmed tortillas.

Nutrition Info:

- (Per serving) Calories 534 | Fat 18g | Sodium 679mg | Carbs 63g | Fiber 8g | Sugar 3g | Protein 27g

Keto Baked Salmon With Pesto

Servings:2 | Cooking Time:18

Ingredients:

- 4 salmon fillets, 2 inches thick
- 2 ounces green pesto
- Salt and black pepper
- ½ tablespoon of canola oil, for greasing
- 1-1/2 cup mayonnaise
- 2 tablespoons Greek yogurt
- Salt and black pepper, to taste

Directions:

1. Rub the salmon with pesto, salt, oil, and black pepper.
2. In a small bowl, whisk together all the green sauce ingredients.
3. Divide the fish fillets between both the baskets.
4. Set zone 1 to air fry mode for 18 minutes at 390 degrees F.
5. Select MATCH button for Zone 2 basket.
6. Once the cooking is done, serve it with green sauce drizzle.
7. Enjoy.

Nutrition Info:

- (Per serving) Calories 1165 | Fat80.7 g| Sodium 1087 mg | Carbs 33.1g | Fiber 0.5g | Sugar11.5 g | Protein 80.6g

Spicy Salmon Fillets

Servings: 6 | Cooking Time: 8 Minutes

Ingredients:

- 900g salmon fillets
- ¾ tsp ground cumin
- 1 tbsp brown sugar
- 2 tbsp steak seasoning
- ¼ tsp cayenne pepper
- ½ tsp ground coriander

Directions:

1. Mix ground cumin, coriander, steak seasoning, brown sugar, and cayenne in a small bowl.
2. Rub salmon fillets with spice mixture.
3. Insert a crisper plate in the Ninja Foodi air fryer baskets.
4. Place the salmon fillets in both baskets.
5. Select zone 1, then select "bake" mode and set the temperature to 360 degrees F for 10 minutes. Press "match" to match zone 2 settings to zone 1. Press "start/stop" to begin.

Nutrition Info:

- (Per serving) Calories 207 | Fat 9.4g |Sodium 68mg | Carbs 1.6g | Fiber 0.1g | Sugar 1.5g | Protein 29.4g

Crusted Tilapia

Servings: 4 | Cooking Time: 17 Minutes.

Ingredients:

- ¾ cup breadcrumbs
- 1 packet dry ranch-style dressing
- 2 ½ tablespoons vegetable oil
- 2 eggs beaten
- 4 tilapia fillets
- Herbs and chilies to garnish

Directions:

1. Thoroughly mix ranch dressing with panko in a bowl.
2. Whisk eggs in a shallow bowl.
3. Dip each fish fillet in the egg, then coat evenly with the panko mixture.
4. Set two coated fillets in each of the crisper plate.
5. Return the crisper plates to the Ninja Foodi Dual Zone Air Fryer.
6. Choose the Air Fry mode for Zone 1 and set the temperature to 390 degrees F and the time to 17 minutes.
7. Select the "MATCH" button to copy the settings for Zone 2.
8. Initiate cooking by pressing the START/STOP button.
9. Serve warm with herbs and chilies.

Nutrition Info:

- (Per serving) Calories 196 | Fat 7.1g |Sodium 492mg | Carbs 21.6g | Fiber 2.9g | Sugar 0.8g | Protein 13.4g

BEEF, PORK, AND LAMB RECIPES

Beef, Pork, And Lamb Recipes

Mustard Pork Chops

Servings: 4 | Cooking Time: 15 Minutes

Ingredients:

- 450g pork chops, boneless
- 55g brown mustard
- 85g honey
- 57g mayonnaise
- 34g BBQ sauce
- Pepper
- Salt

Directions:

1. Coat pork chops with mustard, honey, mayonnaise, BBQ sauce, pepper, and salt in a bowl. Cover and place the bowl in the refrigerator for 1 hour.
2. Insert a crisper plate in the Ninja Foodi air fryer baskets.
3. Place the marinated pork chops in both baskets.
4. Select zone 1, then select "bake" mode and set the temperature to 380 degrees F for 15 minutes. Press "match" and then press "start/stop" to begin. Turn halfway through.

Nutrition Info:

- (Per serving) Calories 496 | Fat 33.1g |Sodium 311mg | Carbs 23.8g | Fiber 0.1g | Sugar 20.4g | Protein 25.7g

Cheesesteak Taquitos

Servings: 8 | Cooking Time: 12 Minutes

Ingredients:

- 1 pack soft corn tortillas
- 136g beef steak strips
- 2 green peppers, sliced
- 1 white onion, chopped
- 1 pkg dry Italian dressing mix
- 10 slices Provolone cheese
- Cooking spray or olive oil

Directions:

1. Mix beef with cooking oil, peppers, onion, and dressing mix in a bowl.
2. Divide the strips in the air fryer baskets.
3. Return the air fryer basket 1 to Zone 1, and basket 2 to Zone 2 of the Ninja Foodi 2-Basket Air Fryer.
4. Choose the "Air Fry" mode for Zone 1 at 375 degrees F and 12 minutes of cooking time.
5. Select the "MATCH COOK" option to copy the settings for Zone 2.
6. Initiate cooking by pressing the START/PAUSE BUTTON.
7. Flip the strips once cooked halfway through.
8. Divide the beef strips in the tortillas and top the beef with a beef slice.
9. Roll the tortillas and serve.

Nutrition Info:

- (Per serving) Calories 410 | Fat 17.8g |Sodium 619mg | Carbs 21g | Fiber 1.4g | Sugar 1.8g | Protein 38.4g

Steak Fajitas With Onions And Peppers

Servings: 6 | Cooking Time: 15 Minutes

Ingredients:

- 1 pound steak
- 1 green bell pepper, sliced
- 1 yellow bell pepper, sliced
- 1 red bell pepper, sliced
- ½ cup sliced white onions
- 1 packet gluten-free fajita seasoning
- Olive oil spray

Directions:

1. Thinly slice the steak against the grain. These should be about ¼-inch slices.
2. Mix the steak with the peppers and onions.
3. Evenly coat with the fajita seasoning.
4. Install a crisper plate in both drawers. Place half the steak mixture in the zone 1 drawer and half in zone 2's, then insert the drawers into the unit.
5. Select zone 1, select AIR FRY, set temperature to 390 degrees F/ 200 degrees C, and set time to 15 minutes. Select MATCH to match zone 2 settings to zone 1. Press the START/STOP button to begin cooking.
6. When the time reaches 10 minutes, press START/STOP to pause the unit. Remove the drawers and flip the steak strips. Re-insert the drawers into the unit and press START/STOP to resume cooking.
7. Serve in warm tortillas.

Nutrition Info:

- (Per serving) Calories 305 | Fat 17g | Sodium 418mg |

Carbs 15g | Fiber 2g | Sugar 4g | Protein 22g

Juicy Pork Chops

Servings: 4 | Cooking Time: 15 Minutes

Ingredients:

- 450g pork chops
- ¼ tsp garlic powder
- 15ml olive oil
- ¼ tsp smoked paprika
- Pepper
- Salt

Directions:

1. In a small bowl, mix the garlic powder, paprika, pepper, and salt.
2. Brush the pork chops with oil and rub with spice mixture.
3. Insert a crisper plate in the Ninja Foodi air fryer baskets.
4. Place the pork chops in both baskets.
5. Select zone 1, then select "bake" mode and set the temperature to 410 degrees F for 15 minutes. Press "match" to match zone 2 settings to zone 1. Press "start/stop" to begin. Turn halfway through.

Nutrition Info:

- (Per serving) Calories 394 | Fat 31.7g |Sodium 118mg | Carbs 0.2g | Fiber 0.1g | Sugar 0.1g | Protein 25.5g

Tomahawk Steak

Servings: 4 | Cooking Time: 12 Minutes

Ingredients:

- 4 tablespoons butter, softened
- 2 cloves garlic, minced
- 2 teaspoons chopped fresh parsley
- 1 teaspoon chopped chives
- 1 teaspoon chopped fresh thyme
- 1 teaspoon chopped fresh rosemary
- 2 (2 pounds each) bone-in ribeye steaks
- Kosher salt, to taste
- Freshly ground black pepper, to taste

Directions:

1. In a small bowl, combine the butter and herbs. Place the mixture in the center of a piece of plastic wrap and roll it into a log. Twist the ends together to keep it tight and refrigerate until hardened, about 20 minutes.
2. Season the steaks on both sides with salt and pepper.
3. Install a crisper plate in both drawers. Place one steak in the zone 1 drawer and one in zone 2's, then insert the drawers into the unit.
4. Select zone 1, select AIR FRY, set temperature to 390 degrees F/ 200 degrees C, and set time to 12 minutes. Select MATCH to match zone 2 settings to zone 1. Press the START/STOP button to begin cooking.
5. When the time reaches 10 minutes, press START/STOP to pause the unit. Remove the drawers and flip the steaks. Add the herb-butter to the tops of the steaks. Re-insert the drawers into the unit and press START/STOP to resume cooking.
6. Serve and enjoy!

Nutrition Info:

- (Per serving) Calories 338 | Fat 21.2g | Sodium 1503mg | Carbs 5.1g | Fiber 0.3g | Sugar 4.6g | Protein 29.3g

Strip Steaks With Hasselback Potatoes

Servings:4 | Cooking Time: 30 Minutes

Ingredients:

- FOR THE STRIP STEAK
- 2 boneless strip steaks (8 ounces each)
- 2 teaspoons vegetable oil
- 1 tablespoon steak seasoning
- FOR THE HASSELBACK POTATOES
- 4 russet potatoes
- 1 tablespoon vegetable oil
- 1 teaspoon kosher salt
- 1 tablespoon salted butter, at room temperature
- 2 teaspoons minced garlic
- 2 teaspoons minced fresh parsley

Directions:

1. To prep the strip steak: Brush both sides of the steaks with the oil and season with the steak seasoning.
2. To prep the Hasselback potatoes: Set a potato on a work surface and lay the handles of two wooden spoons lengthwise on either side of the potato. Make crosswise slits along the potato, spacing them ⅛ inch apart, being careful to not cut the potato completely through (the spoon handles will prevent you from cutting all the way through). Repeat with the remaining potatoes.
3. Rub the potatoes with the oil and season with salt.
4. In a small bowl, mix the butter, garlic, and parsley until smooth.
5. To cook the steak and potatoes: Install a crisper plate in each of the two baskets. Place the steaks in the Zone 1 basket and insert the basket in the unit. Place the potatoes in the Zone 2 basket and insert the basket in the unit.
6. Select Zone 1, select AIR FRY, set the temperature to 375°F, and set the time to 20 minutes.
7. Select Zone 2, select BAKE, set the temperature to

375°F, and set the time to 30 minutes. Select SMART FINISH.

8. Press START/PAUSE to begin cooking.

9. When both timers read 6 minutes, press START/PAUSE. Remove the Zone 1 basket and use silicone-tipped tongs to flip the steaks. Reinsert the basket in the unit. Remove the Zone 2 basket and spread the herb butter into the potatoes, being sure to work the butter in between the slices. Reinsert the basket and press START/PAUSE to resume cooking.

10. When cooking is complete, the steak should be cooked to your liking and the potato soft when pierced with a fork.

11. Remove the steaks from the basket and let rest for 5 minutes before slicing.

Nutrition Info:

- (Per serving) Calories: 361; Total fat: 15g; Saturated fat: 5g; Carbohydrates: 31g; Fiber: 2g; Protein: 25g; Sodium: 694mg

Easy Breaded Pork Chops

Servings: 8 | Cooking Time: 12 Minutes

Ingredients:

- 1 egg
- 118ml milk
- 8 pork chops
- 1 packet ranch seasoning
- 238g breadcrumbs
- Pepper
- Salt

Directions:

1. In a small bowl, whisk the egg and milk.
2. In a separate shallow dish, mix breadcrumbs, ranch seasoning, pepper, and salt.
3. Dip each pork chop in the egg mixture, then coat with breadcrumbs.
4. Insert a crisper plate in the Ninja Foodi air fryer baskets.
5. Place the coated pork chops in both baskets.
6. Select zone 1, then select air fry mode and set the temperature to 360 degrees F for 12 minutes. Press "match" to match zone 2 settings to zone 1. Press "start/stop" to begin. Turn halfway through.

Nutrition Info:

- (Per serving) Calories 378 | Fat 22.2g |Sodium 298mg | Carbs 20.2g | Fiber 1.2g | Sugar 2.4g | Protein 22.8g

Gochujang Brisket

Servings: 6 | Cooking Time: 55 Minutes.

Ingredients:

- ½ tablespoons sweet paprika
- ½ teaspoon toasted sesame oil
- 2 lbs. beef brisket, cut into 4 pieces
- Salt, to taste
- ⅛ cup Gochujang, Korean chili paste
- Black pepper, to taste
- 1 small onion, diced
- 2 garlic cloves, minced
- 1 teaspoon Asian fish sauce
- 1 ½ tablespoons peanut oil, as needed
- ½ tablespoon fresh ginger, grated
- ¼ teaspoon red chili flakes
- ½ cup of water
- 1 tablespoon ketchup
- 1 tablespoon soy sauce

Directions:

1. Thoroughly rub the beef brisket with olive oil, paprika, chili flakes, black pepper, and salt.
2. Cut the brisket in half, then divide the beef in the two crisper plate.
3. Return the crisper plate to the Ninja Foodi Dual Zone Air Fryer.
4. Choose the Air Fry mode for Zone 1 and set the temperature to 390 degrees F and the time to 35 minutes.
5. Select the "MATCH" button to copy the settings for Zone 2.
6. Initiate cooking by pressing the START/STOP button.
7. Flip the brisket halfway through, and resume cooking.
8. Meanwhile, heat oil in a skillet and add ginger, onion, and garlic.
9. Sauté for 5 minutes, then add all the remaining ingredients.
10. Cook the mixture for 15 minutes approximately until well thoroughly mixed.
11. Serve the brisket with this sauce on top.

Nutrition Info:

- (Per serving) Calories 374 | Fat 25g |Sodium 275mg | Carbs 7.3g | Fiber 0g | Sugar 6g | Protein 12.3g

Garlic Sirloin Steak

Servings: 4 | Cooking Time: 10 Minutes

Ingredients:

- 4 sirloin steak
- 30ml olive oil
- 28g steak sauce
- ½ tsp ground coriander
- 1 tsp garlic, minced
- 1 tbsp thyme, chopped
- Pepper
- Salt

Directions:

1. In a bowl, mix steak with thyme, oil, steak sauce, coriander, garlic, pepper, and salt. Cover and set aside for 2 hours.
2. Insert a crisper plate in Ninja Foodi air fryer baskets.
3. Place the marinated steaks in both baskets.
4. Select zone 1 then select air fry mode and set the temperature to 360 degrees F for 10 minutes. Press "match" and then "start/stop" to begin.

Nutrition Info:

- (Per serving) Calories 348 | Fat 18.1g |Sodium 39mg | Carbs 0.7g | Fiber 0.3g | Sugar 0g | Protein 0.1g

Chinese Bbq Pork

Servings:35 | Cooking Time:25

Ingredients:

- 4 tablespoons of soy sauce
- ¼ cup red wine
- 2 tablespoons of oyster sauce
- ¼ tablespoons of hoisin sauce
- ¼ cup honey
- ¼ cup brown sugar
- Pinch of salt
- Pinch of black pepper
- 1 teaspoon of ginger garlic, paste
- 1 teaspoon of five-spice powder
- 1.5 pounds of pork shoulder, sliced

Directions:

1. Take a bowl and mix all the ingredients listed under sauce ingredients.
2. Transfer half of it to a sauce pan and let it cook for 10 minutes.
3. Set it aside.
4. Let the pork marinate in the remaining sauce for 2 hours.
5. Afterward, put the pork slices in the basket and set it to AIRBORIL mode 450 degrees for 25 minutes.
6. Make sure the internal temperature is above 160 degrees F once cooked.
7. If not add a few more minutes to the overall cooking time.
8. Once done, take it out and baste it with prepared sauce.
9. Serve and Enjoy.

Nutrition Info:

- (Per serving) Calories 1239| Fat 73 g| Sodium 2185 mg | Carbs 57.3 g | Fiber 0.4g| Sugar53.7 g | Protein 81.5 g

Beef Cheeseburgers

Servings: 4 | Cooking Time: 13 Minutes.

Ingredients:

- 1 lb. ground beef
- Salt, to taste
- 2 garlic cloves, minced
- 1 tablespoon soy sauce
- Black pepper, to taste
- 4 American cheese slices
- 4 hamburger buns
- Mayonnaise, to serve
- Lettuce, to serve
- Sliced tomatoes, to serve
- Sliced red onion, to serve

Directions:

1. Mix beef with soy sauce and garlic in a large bowl.
2. Make 4 patties of 4 inches in diameter.
3. Rub them with salt and black pepper on both sides.
4. Place the 2 patties in each of the crisper plate.
5. Return the crisper plate to the Ninja Foodi Dual Zone Air Fryer.
6. Choose the Air Fry mode for Zone 1 and set the temperature to 390 degrees F and the time to 13 minutes.
7. Select the "MATCH" button to copy the settings for Zone 2.
8. Initiate cooking by pressing the START/STOP button.
9. Flip each patty once cooked halfway through, and resume cooking.
10. Add each patty to the hamburger buns along with mayo, tomatoes, onions, and lettuce.
11. Serve.

Nutrition Info:

- (Per serving) Calories 437 | Fat 28g |Sodium 1221mg | Carbs 22.3g | Fiber 0.9g | Sugar 8g | Protein 30.3g

Cilantro Lime Steak

Servings: 4 | Cooking Time: 10 Minutes

Ingredients:

- 450g flank steak, sliced
- 1 tsp cumin
- 1 tsp olive oil
- 4 tsp soy sauce
- 12g cilantro, chopped
- ¼ tsp cayenne
- 45ml lime juice
- 2 tsp chilli powder
- ¼ tsp salt

Directions:

1. Add the sliced steak pieces and the remaining ingredients into a zip-lock bag. Seal the bag and place in the refrigerator for 2 hours.
2. Insert a crisper plate in the Ninja Foodi air fryer baskets.
3. Place the marinated steak pieces in both baskets.
4. Select zone 1, then select "air fry" mode and set the temperature to 380 degrees F for 10 minutes. Press "match" to match zone 2 settings to zone 1. Press "start/stop" to begin.

Nutrition Info:

- (Per serving) Calories 240 | Fat 11g |Sodium 524mg | Carbs 1.5g | Fiber 0.6g | Sugar 0.2g | Protein 32.2g

Air Fryer Meatloaves

Servings: 4 | Cooking Time: 22 Minutes.

Ingredients:

- ⅓ cup milk
- 2 tablespoons basil pesto
- 1 egg, beaten
- 1 garlic clove, minced
- ¼ teaspoons black pepper
- 1 lb. ground beef
- ⅓ cup panko bread crumbs
- 8 pepperoni slices
- ½ cup marinara sauce, warmed
- 1 tablespoon fresh basil, chopped

Directions:

1. Mix pesto, milk, egg, garlic, and black pepper in a medium-sized bowl.
2. Stir in ground beef and bread crumbs, then mix.
3. Make the 4 small-sized loaves with this mixture and top them with 2 pepperoni slices.
4. Press the slices into the meatloaves.
5. Place the meatloaves in the two crisper plates.
6. Return the crisper plate to the Ninja Foodi Dual Zone Air Fryer.
7. Choose the Air Fry mode for Zone 1 and set the temperature to 390 degrees F and the time to 22 minutes.
8. Select the "MATCH" button to copy the settings for Zone 2.
9. Initiate cooking by pressing the START/STOP button.
10. Top them with marinara sauce and basil to serve.
11. Serve warm.

Nutrition Info:

- (Per serving) Calories 316 | Fat 12.2g |Sodium 587mg | Carbs 12.2g | Fiber 1g | Sugar 1.8g | Protein 25.8g

Jerk-rubbed Pork Loin With Carrots And Sage

Servings: 4 | Cooking Time: 35 Minutes

Ingredients:

- 1½ pounds pork loin
- 3 teaspoons canola oil, divided
- 2 tablespoons jerk seasoning
- 1-pound carrots, peeled, cut into 1-inch pieces
- 1 tablespoon honey
- ½ teaspoon kosher salt
- ½ teaspoon chopped fresh sage

Directions:

1. Place the pork loin in a pan or a dish with a high wall. Using a paper towel, pat the meat dry.
2. Rub 2 teaspoons of canola oil evenly over the pork with your hands. Then spread the jerk seasoning evenly over it with your hands.
3. Allow the pork loin to marinate for at least 10 minutes or up to 8 hours in the refrigerator after wrapping it in plastic wrap or sealing it in a plastic bag.
4. Toss the carrots with the remaining canola oil and ½ teaspoon of salt in a medium mixing bowl.
5. Place a crisper plate in each of the drawers. Put the marinated pork loin in the zone 1 drawer and place it in the unit. Place the carrots in the zone 2 drawer and place the drawer in the unit.
6. Select zone 1 and select AIR FRY. Set the temperature to 390 degrees F/ 200 degrees C and the time setting to 25 minutes. Select zone 2 and select AIR FRY. Set the temperature to 390 degrees F/ 200 degrees C and the time setting to 16 minutes. Select SYNC. Press START/STOP to begin cooking.
7. Check the pork loin for doneness after the zones have finished cooking. When the internal temperature of the loin hits 145°F on an instant-read thermometer, the pork is ready.
8. Allow the pork loin to rest for at least 5 minutes on

a plate or cutting board.

9. Combine the carrots and sage in a mixing bowl.
10. When the pork loin has rested, slice it into the desired thickness of slices and serve with the carrots.

Nutrition Info:

- (Per serving) Calories 500 | Fat 19.8g | Sodium 680mg | Carbs 50.1g | Fiber 4.1g | Sugar 0g | Protein 27.9g

Steak And Mashed Creamy Potatoes

Servings:1 | Cooking Time:45

Ingredients:

- 2 Russet potatoes, peeled and cubed
- ¼ cup butter, divided
- 1/3 cup heavy cream
- ½ cup shredded cheddar cheese
- Salt and black pepper, to taste
- 1 New York strip steak, about a pound
- 1 teaspoon of olive oil
- Oil spray, for greasing

Directions:

1. Rub the potatoes with salt and a little amount of olive oil about a teaspoon.
2. Next, season the steak with salt and black pepper.
3. Place the russet potatoes in a zone 1 basket.
4. Oil spray the steak from both sides and then place it in the zone 2 basket.
5. Set zone 1 to AIR fry mode for 45 minutes at 390 degrees F.
6. Set the zone 2 basket, at 12 minutes at 375 degrees F.
7. Hot start and Lethe ninja foodie do its magic.
8. One the cooking cycle completes, take out the steak and potatoes.
9. Mash the potatoes and then add butter, heavy cream, and cheese along with salt and black pepper.
10. Serve the mashed potatoes with steak.
11. Enjoy.

Nutrition Info:

- (Per serving) Calories1932 | Fat 85.2g| Sodium 3069mg | Carbs 82g | Fiber10.3 g| Sugar 5.3g | Protein 22.5g

Beef Ribs I

Servings:2 | Cooking Time:15

Ingredients:

- 4 tablespoons of barbecue spice rub
- 1 tablespoon kosher salt and black pepper
- 3 tablespoons brown sugar
- 2 pounds of beef ribs (3-3 1/2 pounds), cut in thirds
- 1 cup barbecue sauce

Directions:

1. In a small bowl, add salt, pepper, brown sugar, and BBQ spice rub.
2. Grease the ribs with oil spray from both sides and then rub it with a spice mixture.
3. Divide the ribs amongst the basket and set it to AIR FRY MODE at 375 degrees F for 15 minutes.
4. Hit start and let the air fryer cook the ribs.
5. Once done, serve with the coating BBQ sauce.

Nutrition Info:

- (Per serving) Calories1081 | Fat 28.6 g| Sodium 1701mg | Carbs 58g | Fiber 0.8g| Sugar 45.7g | Protein 138 g

Asian Pork Skewers

Servings: 4 | Cooking Time: 25 Minutes

Ingredients:

- 450g pork shoulder, sliced
- 30g ginger, peeled and crushed
- ½ tablespoon crushed garlic
- 67½ml soy sauce
- 22½ml honey
- 22½ml rice vinegar
- 10ml toasted sesame oil
- 8 skewers

Directions:

1. Pound the pork slices with a mallet.
2. Mix ginger, garlic, soy sauce, honey, rice vinegar, and sesame oil in a bowl.
3. Add pork slices to the marinade and mix well to coat.
4. Cover and marinate the pork for 30 minutes.
5. Thread the pork on the wooden skewers and place them in the air fryer baskets.
6. Return the air fryer basket 1 to Zone 1, and basket 2 to Zone 2 of the Ninja Foodi 2-Basket Air Fryer.
7. Choose the "Air Fry" mode for Zone 1 and set the temperature to 350 degrees F and 25 minutes of cooking time.
8. Select the "MATCH COOK" option to copy the settings for Zone 2.
9. Initiate cooking by pressing the START/PAUSE BUTTON.
10. Flip the skewers once cooked halfway through.
11. Serve warm.

Nutrition Info:

- (Per serving) Calories 400 | Fat 32g |Sodium 721mg | Carbs 2.6g | Fiber 0g | Sugar 0g | Protein 27.4g

Meatballs

Servings: 4 | Cooking Time: 20 Minutes

Ingredients:

- 450g ground beef
- 59ml milk
- 45g parmesan cheese, grated
- 50g breadcrumbs
- ½ tsp Italian seasoning
- 2 garlic cloves, minced
- Pepper
- Salt

Directions:

1. In a bowl, mix the meat and remaining ingredients until well combined.
2. Insert a crisper plate in the Ninja Foodi air fryer baskets.
3. Make small balls from the meat mixture and place them in both baskets.
4. Select zone 1, then select "air fry" mode and set the temperature to 375 degrees F for 15 minutes. Press "match" and "start/stop" to begin.

Nutrition Info:

- (Per serving) Calories 426 | Fat 17.3g |Sodium 820mg | Carbs 11.1g | Fiber 0.7g | Sugar 1.6g | Protein 48.8g

Ham Burger Patties

Servings:2 | Cooking Time:17

Ingredients:

- 1 pound of ground beef
- Salt and pepper, to taste
- ½ teaspoon of red chili powder
- ¼ teaspoon of coriander powder
- 2 tablespoons of chopped onion
- 1 green chili, chopped
- Oil spray for greasing
- 2 large potato wedges

Directions:

1. Oil greases the air fryer baskets with oil spray.
2. Add potato wedges in the zone 1 basket.
3. Take a bowl and add minced beef in it and add salt, pepper, chili powder, coriander powder, green chili, and chopped onion.
4. mix well and make two burger patties with wet hands place the two patties in the air fryer zone 2 basket.
5. put the basket inside the air fryer.
6. now, set time for zone 1 for 12 minutes using AIR FRY mode at 400 degrees F.
7. Select the MATCH button for zone 2.
8. once the time of cooking complete, take out the baskets.
9. flip the patties and shake the potatoes wedges.
10. again, set time of zone 1 basket for 4 minutes at 400 degrees F
11. Select the MATCH button for the second basket.
12. Once it's done, serve and enjoy.

Nutrition Info:

- (Per serving) Calories875 | Fat21.5g | Sodium 622mg | Carbs 88g | Fiber10.9 g| Sugar 3.4g | Protein 78.8g

Mongolian Beef With Sweet Chili Brussels Sprouts

Servings:4 | Cooking Time: 20 Minutes

Ingredients:

- FOR THE MONGOLIAN BEEF
- 1 pound flank steak, cut into thin strips
- 1 tablespoon olive oil
- 2 tablespoons cornstarch
- ½ cup reduced-sodium soy sauce
- ½ cup packed light brown sugar
- 1 tablespoon chili paste (optional)
- 1 tablespoon minced garlic
- 1 tablespoon minced fresh ginger
- 2 scallions, chopped
- FOR THE BRUSSELS SPROUTS
- 1 pound Brussels sprouts, halved lengthwise
- 1 tablespoon olive oil
- ½ cup gochujang sauce
- 2 tablespoons rice vinegar
- 1 tablespoon reduced-sodium soy sauce
- 1 tablespoon light brown sugar
- 1 teaspoon fresh garlic

Directions:

1. To prep the Mongolian beef: In a large bowl, combine the flank steak and olive oil and toss to coat. Add the cornstarch and toss to coat.
2. In a small bowl, whisk together the soy sauce, brown sugar, chili paste (if using), garlic, and ginger. Set the soy sauce mixture aside.
3. To prep the Brussels sprouts: In a large bowl, combine the Brussels sprouts and oil and toss to coat.
4. In a small bowl, whisk together the gochujang sauce, vinegar, soy sauce, brown sugar, and garlic. Set the chili sauce mixture aside.
5. To cook the beef and Brussels sprouts: Install a crisper plate in each of the two baskets. Place the beef in the Zone 1 basket and insert the basket in the unit. Place the Brussels sprouts in the Zone 2 basket and insert the basket in the unit.
6. Select Zone 1, select AIR FRY, set the temperature to 390°F, and set the time to 15 minutes.

7. Select Zone 2, select AIR FRY, set the temperature to 400°F, and set the time to 20 minutes. Select SMART FINISH.
8. Press START/PAUSE to begin cooking.
9. When both timers read 5 minutes, press START/PAUSE. Remove the Zone 1 basket, add the reserved soy sauce mixture and the scallions, and toss with the beef. Reinsert the basket. Remove the Zone 2 basket, add the reserved chili sauce mixture, and toss with the Brussels sprouts. Reinsert the basket and press START/PAUSE to resume cooking.
10. When cooking is complete, the steak should be cooked through and the Brussels sprouts tender and slightly caramelized. Serve warm.

Nutrition Info:

- (Per serving) Calories: 481; Total fat: 16g; Saturated fat: 4.5g; Carbohydrates: 60g; Fiber: 5g; Protein: 27g; Sodium: 2,044mg

Pigs In A Blanket With Spinach-artichoke Stuffed Mushrooms

Servings:4 | Cooking Time: 15 Minutes

Ingredients:

- FOR THE PIGS IN A BLANKET
- Half an 8-ounce tube refrigerated crescent roll dough
- 4 hot dogs
- ½ teaspoon everything bagel seasoning (optional)
- FOR THE STUFFED MUSHROOMS
- 1 cup frozen chopped spinach, thawed and drained
- 1 (14-ounce) can artichoke hearts, drained and chopped
- 2 ounces (¼ cup) cream cheese, at room temperature
- ¼ cup grated Parmesan cheese
- ½ teaspoon garlic powder
- 1 (8-ounce) package whole cremini mushrooms, stems removed

Directions:

1. To prep the pigs in a blanket: Unroll the crescent roll dough. It will be scored into 4 triangular pieces, but leave them in place and pinch together at the seams to form 1 large square of dough. Cut the dough into 4 strips.
2. Wrap one strip of dough around each hot dog, starting with a short end of the strips and wrapping in a spiral motion around the hot dog. If desired, sprinkle each pig in a blanket with everything bagel seasoning.
3. To prep the stuffed mushrooms: In a medium bowl, combine the spinach, artichoke hearts, cream cheese, Parmesan, and garlic powder. Stuff about 1 tablespoon of filling into each mushroom cap.
4. To cook the pigs in a blanket and mushrooms: Install a crisper plate in each of the two baskets. Place the pigs in a blanket in the Zone 1 basket and insert the basket in the unit. Place the mushrooms in the Zone 2 basket and insert the basket in the unit.
5. Select Zone 1, select AIR FRY, set the temperature to 370°F, and set the time to 8 minutes.
6. Select Zone 2, select BAKE, set the temperature to 370°F, and set the time to 15 minutes. Select SMART FINISH.
7. Press START/PAUSE to begin cooking.
8. When cooking is complete, the crescent roll dough should be cooked through and golden brown, and the mushrooms should be tender.

Nutrition Info:

- (Per serving) Calories: 371; Total fat: 25g; Saturated fat: 11g; Carbohydrates: 22g; Fiber: 2.5g; Protein: 14g; Sodium: 1,059mg

Curry-crusted Lamb Chops With Baked Brown Sugar Acorn Squash

Servings:4 | Cooking Time: 20 Minutes

Ingredients:

- FOR THE LAMB CHOPS
- 4 lamb loin chops (4 ounces each)
- 1 tablespoon olive oil
- 2 teaspoons curry powder
- ¼ teaspoon kosher salt
- FOR THE ACORN SQUASH
- 2 small acorn squash
- 4 teaspoons dark brown sugar
- 2 teaspoons salted butter
- ⅛ teaspoon kosher salt

Directions:

1. To prep the lamb chops: Brush both sides of the lamb chops with the oil and season with the curry powder and salt.
2. To prep the acorn squash: Cut the squash in half through the stem end and remove the seeds. Place 1 teaspoon of brown sugar and ½ teaspoon of butter into the well of each squash half.
3. To cook the lamb and squash: Install a crisper plate in each of the two baskets. Place the lamb chops in the Zone 1 basket and insert the basket in the unit. Place the squash cut-side up in the Zone 2 basket and

insert the basket in the unit.
4. Select Zone 1, select AIR FRY, set the temperature to 400°F, and set the timer to 15 minutes.
5. Select Zone 2, select BAKE, set the temperature to 400°F, and set the time to 20 minutes. Select SMART FINISH.
6. Press START/PAUSE to begin cooking.
7. When both timers read 5 minutes, press START/PAUSE. Remove the Zone 1 basket and use a pair of silicone-tipped tongs to flip the lamb chops. Reinsert the basket in the unit. Remove the Zone 2 basket and spoon the melted butter and sugar over the top edges of the squash. Reinsert the basket and press START/PAUSE to resume cooking.
8. When cooking is complete, the lamb should be cooked to your liking and the squash soft when pierced with a fork.
9. Remove the lamb chops from the basket and let rest for 5 minutes. Season the acorn squash with salt before serving.

Nutrition Info:

- (Per serving) Calories: 328; Total fat: 19g; Saturated fat: 7.5g; Carbohydrates: 23g; Fiber: 3g; Protein: 16g; Sodium: 172mg

Zucchini Pork Skewers

Servings: 4 | Cooking Time: 23 Minutes.

Ingredients:

- 1 large zucchini, cut 1" pieces
- 1 lb. boneless pork belly, cut into cubes
- 1 onion yellow, diced in squares
- 1 ½ cups grape tomatoes
- 1 garlic clove minced
- 1 lemon, juice only
- ¼ cup olive oil
- 2 tablespoons balsamic vinegar
- 1 teaspoon oregano
- olive oil spray

Directions:

1. Mix together balsamic vinegar, garlic, oregano lemon juice, and ¼ cup of olive oil in a suitable bowl.
2. Then toss in diced pork pieces and mix well to coat.
3. Leave the seasoned pork to marinate for 60 minutes in the refrigerator.
4. Take suitable wooden skewers for your Ninja Foodi Dual Zone Air Fryer's drawer, and then thread marinated pork and vegetables on each skewer in an alternating manner.
5. Place half of the skewers in each of the crisper plate and spray them with cooking oil.
6. Return the crisper plate to the Ninja Foodi Dual Zone Air Fryer.
7. Choose the Air Fry mode for Zone 1 and set the temperature to 390 degrees F and the time to 23 minutes.
8. Select the "MATCH" button to copy the settings for Zone 2.
9. Initiate cooking by pressing the START/STOP button.
10. Flip the skewers once cooked halfway through, and resume cooking.
11. Serve warm.

Nutrition Info:

- (Per serving) Calories 459 | Fat 17.7g |Sodium 1516mg | Carbs 1.7g | Fiber 0.5g | Sugar 0.4g | Protein 69.2g

Spicy Lamb Chops

Servings:4 | Cooking Time:15

Ingredients:

- 12 lamb chops, bone-in
- Salt and black pepper, to taste
- ½ teaspoon of lemon zest
- 1 tablespoon of lemon juice
- 1 teaspoon of paprika
- 1 teaspoon of garlic powder
- ½ teaspoon of Italian seasoning
- ¼ teaspoon of onion powder

Directions:

1. Add the lamb chops to the bowl and sprinkle salt, garlic powder, Italian seasoning, onion powder, black pepper, lemon zest, lemon juice, and paprika.
2. Rub the chops well, and divide it between both the baskets of the air fryer.
3. Set zone 1 basket to 400 degrees F, for 15 minutes at AIR FRY mode.
4. Select MATCH for zone2 basket.
5. After 10 minutes, take out the baskets and flip the chops cook for the remaining minutes, and then serve.

Nutrition Info:

- (Per serving) Calories 787| Fat 45.3g| Sodium1 mg | Carbs 16.1g | Fibero.3g | Sugar 0.4g | Protein 75.3g

Beef Ribs Ii

Servings:2 | Cooking Time:1

Ingredients:

- ¼ cup olive oil
- 4 garlic cloves, minced
- ½ cup white wine vinegar
- ¼ cup soy sauce, reduced-sodium
- ¼ cup Worcestershire sauce
- 1 lemon juice
- Salt and black pepper, to taste
- 2 tablespoons of Italian seasoning
- 1 teaspoon of smoked paprika
- 2 tablespoons of mustard
- ½ cup maple syrup
- Meat Ingredients:
- Oil spray, for greasing
- 8 beef ribs lean

Directions:

1. Take a large bowl and add all the ingredients under marinade ingredients.
2. Put the marinade in a zip lock bag and add ribs to it.
3. Let it sit for 4 hours.
4. Now take out the basket of air fryer and grease the baskets with oil spray.
5. Now dived the ribs among two baskets.
6. Set it to AIR fry mode at 220 degrees F for 30 minutes.
7. Select Pause and take out the baskets.
8. Afterward, flip the ribs and cook for 30 minutes at 250 degrees F.
9. Once done, serve the juicy and tender ribs.
10. Enjoy.

Nutrition Info:

- (Per serving) Calories 1927| Fat116g| Sodium 1394mg | Carbs 35.2g | Fiber 1.3g| Sugar29 g | Protein 172.3g

Pork Chops With Brussels Sprouts

Servings: 4 | Cooking Time: 15 Minutes.

Ingredients:

- 4 bone-in center-cut pork chop
- Cooking spray
- Salt, to taste
- Black pepper, to taste
- 2 teaspoons olive oil
- 2 teaspoons pure maple syrup
- 2 teaspoons Dijon mustard
- 6 ounces Brussels sprouts, quartered

Directions:

1. Rub pork chop with salt, ¼ teaspoons black pepper, and cooking spray.
2. Toss Brussels sprouts with mustard, syrup, oil, ¼ teaspoon of black pepper in a medium bowl.
3. Add pork chop to the crisper plate of Zone 1 of the Ninja Foodi Dual Zone Air Fryer.
4. Return the crisper plate to the Ninja Foodi Dual Zone Air Fryer.
5. Choose the Air Fry mode for Zone 1 and set the temperature to 400 degrees F and the time to 15 minutes.
6. Add the Brussels sprouts to the crisper plate of Zone 2 and return it to the unit.
7. Choose the Air Fry mode for Zone 2 with 350 degrees F and the time to 13 minutes.
8. Press the SYNC button to sync the finish time for both Zones.
9. Initiate cooking by pressing the START/STOP button.
10. Serve warm and fresh

Nutrition Info:

- (Per serving) Calories 336 | Fat 27.1g |Sodium 66mg | Carbs 1.1g | Fiber 0.4g | Sugar 0.2g | Protein 19.7g

POULTRY RECIPES

Poultry Recipes

Chicken Parmesan

Servings: 4 | Cooking Time: 20 Minutes

Ingredients:

- 2 large eggs
- ½ cup seasoned breadcrumbs
- 1⁄3 cup grated parmesan cheese
- ¼ teaspoon pepper
- 4 boneless, skinless chicken breast halves (6 ounces each)
- 1 cup pasta sauce
- 1 cup shredded mozzarella cheese
- Chopped fresh basil (optional)

Directions:

1. Lightly beat the eggs in a small bowl.
2. Combine the breadcrumbs, parmesan cheese, and pepper in a shallow bowl.
3. After dipping the chicken in the egg, coat it in the crumb mixture.
4. Install a crisper plate in both drawers. Place half the chicken breasts in the zone 1 drawer and half in zone 2's, then insert the drawers into the unit.
5. Select zone 1, select AIR FRY, set temperature to 390 degrees F/ 200 degrees C, and set time to 20 minutes. Select MATCH to match zone 2 settings to zone 1. Press the START/STOP button to begin cooking.
6. When the time reaches 10 minutes, press START/STOP to pause the unit. Remove the drawers and flip the chicken. Re-insert the drawers into the unit and press START/STOP to resume cooking.
7. When cooking is complete, remove the chicken.

Nutrition Info:

- (Per serving) Calories 293 | Fat 15.8g | Sodium 203mg | Carbs 11.1g | Fiber 2.4g | Sugar 8.7g | Protein 29g

Maple-mustard Glazed Turkey Tenderloin With Apple And Sage Stuffing

Servings:4 | Cooking Time: 35 Minutes

Ingredients:

- FOR THE TURKEY TENDERLOIN
- 2 tablespoons maple syrup
- 1 tablespoon unsalted butter, at room temperature
- 1 tablespoon Dijon mustard
- ½ teaspoon kosher salt
- ½ teaspoon freshly ground black pepper
- 1½ pounds turkey tenderloin
- FOR THE STUFFING
- 6 ounces seasoned stuffing mix
- 1½ cups chicken broth
- 1 apple, peeled, cored, and diced
- 1 tablespoon chopped fresh sage
- 2 teaspoons unsalted butter, cut into several pieces

Directions:

1. To prep the turkey tenderloin: In a small bowl, mix the maple syrup, butter, mustard, salt, and black pepper until smooth. Spread the maple mixture over the entire turkey tenderloin.
2. To prep the stuffing: In the Zone 2 basket, combine the stuffing mix and chicken broth. Stir well to ensure the bread is fully moistened. Stir in the apple and sage. Scatter the butter on top.
3. To cook the turkey and stuffing: Install a crisper plate in the Zone 1 basket. Place the turkey tenderloin in the basket and insert the basket in the unit. Insert the Zone 2 basket in the unit.
4. Select Zone 1, select AIR FRY, set the temperature to 390°F, and set the time to 35 minutes.
5. Select Zone 2, select BAKE, set the temperature to 340°F, and set the time to 20 minutes. Select SMART FINISH.
6. Press START/PAUSE to begin cooking.
7. When the Zone 2 timer reads 10 minutes, press START/PAUSE. Remove the basket and stir the stuffing. Reinsert the basket and press START/PAUSE to resume cooking.
8. When cooking is complete, the turkey will be cooked through (an instant-read thermometer should read 165°F) and the stuffing will have absorbed all the liquid and be slightly crisp on top. Serve warm.

Nutrition Info:

- (Per serving) Calories: 455; Total fat: 10g; Saturated fat: 3g; Carbohydrates: 42g; Fiber: 2.5g; Protein: 46g; Sodium: 1,230mg

Chili Chicken Wings

Servings: 4 | Cooking Time: 43 Minutes.

Ingredients:

- 8 chicken wings drumettes
- cooking spray
- ⅛ cup low-fat buttermilk
- ¼ cup almond flour
- McCormick Chicken Seasoning to taste
- Thai Chili Marinade
- 1 ½ tablespoons low-sodium soy sauce
- ½ teaspoon ginger, minced
- 1 ½ garlic cloves
- 1 green onion
- ½ teaspoon rice wine vinegar
- ½ tablespoon Sriracha sauce
- ½ tablespoon sesame oil

Directions:

1. Put all the ingredients for the marinade in the blender and blend them for 1 minute.
2. Keep this marinade aside. Pat dry the washed chicken and place it in the Ziploc bag.
3. Add buttermilk, chicken seasoning, and zip the bag.
4. Shake the bag well, then refrigerator for 30 minutes for marination.
5. Remove the chicken drumettes from the marinade, then dredge them through dry flour.
6. Spread the drumettes in the two crisper plate and spray them with cooking oil.
7. Return the crisper plate to the Ninja Foodi Dual Zone Air Fryer.
8. Choose the Air Fry mode for Zone 1 and set the temperature to 390 degrees F and the time to 43 minutes.
9. Select the "MATCH" button to copy the settings for Zone 2.
10. Initiate cooking by pressing the START/STOP button.
11. Toss the drumettes once cooked halfway through.
12. Now brush the chicken pieces with Thai chili sauce and then resume cooking.
13. Serve warm.

Nutrition Info:

- (Per serving) Calories 223 | Fat 11.7g |Sodium 721mg | Carbs 13.6g | Fiber 0.7g | Sugar 8g | Protein 15.7g

Sesame Ginger Chicken

Servings: 4 | Cooking Time: 30 Minutes

Ingredients:

- 4 ounces green beans
- 1 tablespoon canola oil
- 1½ pounds boneless, skinless chicken breasts
- ⅓ cup prepared sesame-ginger sauce
- Kosher salt, to taste
- Black pepper, to taste

Directions:

1. Toss the green beans with a teaspoon of salt and pepper in a medium mixing bowl.
2. Place a crisper plate in each drawer. Place the green beans in the zone 1 drawer and insert it into the unit. Place the chicken breasts in the zone 2 drawer and place it inside the unit.
3. Select zone 1, then AIR FRY, and set the temperature to 390 degrees F/ 200 degrees C with a 10-minute timer. Select zone 2, then AIR FRY, and set the temperature to 390 degrees F/ 200 degrees C with an 18-minute timer. Select SYNC. To begin cooking, press the START/STOP button.
4. Press START/STOP to pause the unit when the zone 2 timer reaches 9 minutes. Remove the chicken from the drawer and toss it in the sesame ginger sauce. To resume cooking, re-insert the drawer into the unit and press START/STOP.
5. When cooking is complete, serve the chicken breasts and green beans straight away.

Nutrition Info:

- (Per serving) Calories 143 | Fat 7g | Sodium 638mg | Carbs 11.6g | Fiber 1.4g | Sugar 8.5g | Protein 11.1g

Chicken Breast Strips

Servings:2 | Cooking Time:22

Ingredients:

- 2 large organic egg
- 1-ounce buttermilk
- 1 cup of cornmeal
- ¼ cup all-purpose flour
- Salt and black pepper, to taste
- 1 pound of chicken breasts, cut into strips
- 2 tablespoons of oil bay seasoning
- oil spray, for greasing

Directions:

1. Take a medium bowl and whisk eggs with buttermilk.
2. In a separate large bowl mix flour, cornmeal, salt, black pepper, and oil bay seasoning.
3. First, dip the chicken breast strip in egg wash and then dredge into the flour mixture.

4. Coat the strip all over and layer on both the baskets that are already grease with oil spray.
5. Grease the chicken breast strips with oil spray as well.
6. Set the zone 1 basket to AIR FRY mode at 400 degrees F for 22 minutes.
7. Select the MATCH button for zone 2.
8. Hit the start button to let the cooking start.
9. Once the cooking cycle is done, serve.

Nutrition Info:

- (Per serving) Calories 788| Fat25g| Sodium835 mg | Carbs60g | Fiber 4.9g| Sugar1.5g | Protein79g

Crumbed Chicken Katsu

Servings: 4 | Cooking Time: 26 Minutes.

Ingredients:

- 1 lb. boneless chicken breast, cut in half
- 2 large eggs, beaten
- 1 ½ cups panko bread crumbs
- Salt and black pepper ground to taste
- Cooking spray
- Sauce:
- 1 tablespoon sugar
- 2 tablespoons soy sauce
- 1 tablespoon sherry
- ½ cup ketchup
- 2 teaspoons Worcestershire sauce
- 1 teaspoon garlic, minced

Directions:

1. Mix soy sauce, ketchup, sherry, sugar, garlic, and Worcestershire sauce in a mixing bowl.
2. Keep this katsu aside for a while.
3. Rub the chicken pieces with salt and black pepper.
4. Whisk eggs in a shallow dish and spread breadcrumbs in another tray.
5. Dip the chicken in the egg mixture and coat them with breadcrumbs.
6. Place the coated chicken in the two crisper plates and spray them with cooking spray.
7. Return the crisper plate to the Ninja Foodi Dual Zone Air Fryer.
8. Choose the Air Fry mode for Zone 1 and set the temperature to 390 degrees F and the time to 26 minutes.
9. Select the "MATCH" button to copy the settings for Zone 2.
10. Initiate cooking by pressing the START/STOP button.
11. Flip the chicken once cooked halfway through, then resume cooking.
12. Serve warm with the sauce.

Nutrition Info:

- (Per serving) Calories 220 | Fat 1.7g |Sodium 178mg | Carbs 1.7g | Fiber 0.2g | Sugar 0.2g | Protein 32.9g

Veggie Stuffed Chicken Breasts

Servings: 2 | Cooking Time: 10 Minutes.

Ingredients:

- 4 teaspoons chili powder
- 4 teaspoons ground cumin
- 1 skinless, boneless chicken breast
- 2 teaspoons chipotle flakes
- 2 teaspoons Mexican oregano
- Salt and black pepper, to taste
- ½ red bell pepper, julienned
- ½ onion, julienned
- 1 fresh jalapeno pepper, julienned
- 2 teaspoons corn oil
- ½ lime, juiced

Directions:

1. Slice the chicken breast in half horizontally.
2. Pound each chicken breast with a mallet into ¼ inch thickness.
3. Rub the pounded chicken breast with black pepper, salt, oregano, chipotle flakes, cumin, and chili powder.
4. Add ½ of bell pepper, jalapeno, and onion on top of each chicken breast piece.
5. Roll the chicken to wrap the filling inside and insert toothpicks to seal.
6. Place the rolls in crisper plate and spray them with cooking oil.
7. Return the crisper plate to the Ninja Foodi Dual Zone Air Fryer.
8. Choose the Air Fry mode for Zone 1 and set the temperature to 360 degrees F and the time to 10 minutes.
9. Initiate cooking by pressing the START/STOP button.
10. Serve warm.

Nutrition Info:

- (Per serving) Calories 351 | Fat 11g |Sodium 150mg | Carbs 3.3g | Fiber 0.2g | Sugar 1g | Protein 33.2g

Delicious Chicken Skewers

Servings: 4 | Cooking Time: 15 Minutes

Ingredients:

- 900g chicken thighs, cut into cubes
- 45ml fresh lime juice
- 59ml coconut milk
- 2 tbsp Thai red curry
- 35ml maple syrup
- 120ml tamari soy sauce

Directions:

1. Add chicken and remaining ingredients into the bowl and mix well.
2. Cover the bowl and place in the refrigerator for 2 hours.
3. Thread the marinated chicken onto the soaked skewers.
4. Insert a crisper plate in the Ninja Foodi air fryer baskets.
5. Place the chicken skewers in both baskets.
6. Select zone 1 then select "air fry" mode and set the temperature to 360 degrees F for 15 minutes. Press "match" to match zone 2 settings to zone 1. Press "start/stop" to begin.

Nutrition Info:

- (Per serving) Calories 526 | Fat 20.5g |Sodium 2210mg | Carbs 12.9g | Fiber 0.6g | Sugar 10g | Protein 69.7g

Buffalo Chicken

Servings: 4 | Cooking Time: 22 Minutes

Ingredients:

- ½ cup plain fat-free Greek yogurt
- ¼ cup egg substitute
- 1 tablespoon plus 1 teaspoon hot sauce
- 1 cup panko bread-crumbs
- 1 tablespoon sweet paprika
- 1 tablespoon garlic pepper seasoning
- 1 tablespoon cayenne pepper
- 1-pound skinless, boneless chicken breasts, cut into 1-inch strips

Directions:

1. Combine the Greek yogurt, egg substitute, and hot sauce in a mixing bowl.
2. In a separate bowl, combine the panko breadcrumbs, paprika, garlic powder, and cayenne pepper.
3. Dip the chicken strips in the yogurt mixture, then coat them in the breadcrumb mixture.
4. Install a crisper plate in both drawers. Place the chicken strips into the drawers and then insert the drawers into the unit.
5. Select zone 1, select AIR FRY, set temperature to 390 degrees F/ 200 degrees C, and set time to 22 minutes. Select MATCH to match zone 2 settings to zone 1. Press the START/STOP button to begin cooking.
6. When cooking is complete, serve immediately.

Nutrition Info:

- (Per serving) Calories 234 | Fat 15.8g | Sodium 696mg | Carbs 22.1g | Fiber 1.1g | Sugar 1.7g | Protein 31.2g

Teriyaki Chicken Skewers

Servings: 4 | Cooking Time: 16 Minutes

Ingredients:

- 455g boneless chicken thighs, cubed
- 237ml teriyaki marinade
- 16 small wooden skewers
- Sesame seeds for rolling
- Teriyaki Marinade
- ⅓ cup soy sauce
- 59ml chicken broth
- ½ orange, juiced
- 2 tablespoons brown sugar
- 1 teaspoon ginger, grated
- 1 clove garlic, grated

Directions:

1. Blend teriyaki marinade ingredients in a blender.
2. Add chicken and its marinade to a Ziplock bag.
3. Seal this bag, shake it well and refrigerate for 30 minutes.
4. Thread the chicken on the wooden skewers.
5. Place these skewers in the air fryer baskets.
6. Return the air fryer basket 1 to Zone 1, and basket 2 to Zone 2 of the Ninja Foodi 2-Basket Air Fryer.
7. Choose the "Air Fry" mode for Zone 1 at 350 degrees F and 16 minutes of cooking time.
8. Select the "MATCH COOK" option to copy the settings for Zone 2.
9. Initiate cooking by pressing the START/PAUSE BUTTON.
10. Flip the skewers once cooked halfway through.
11. Garnish with sesame seeds.
12. Serve warm.

Nutrition Info:

- (Per serving) Calories 456 | Fat 16.4g |Sodium 1321mg | Carbs 19.2g | Fiber 2.2g | Sugar 4.2g | Protein 55.2g

Crispy Ranch Nuggets

Servings: 4 | Cooking Time: 10 Minutes

Ingredients:

- 1 pound chicken tenders, cut into 1½–2-inch pieces
- 1 (1-ounce) sachet dry ranch salad dressing mix
- 2 tablespoons flour
- 1 egg
- 1 cup panko breadcrumbs
- Olive oil cooking spray

Directions:

1. Toss the chicken with the ranch seasoning in a large mixing bowl. Allow for 5–10 minutes of resting time.
2. Fill a resalable bag halfway with the flour.
3. Crack the egg into a small bowl and lightly beat it.
4. Spread the breadcrumbs onto a dish.
5. Toss the chicken in the bag to coat it. Dip the chicken in the egg mixture lightly, allowing excess to drain off. Roll the chicken pieces in the breadcrumbs, pressing them in, so they stick. Lightly spray with the cooking spray.
6. Install a crisper plate in both drawers. Place half the chicken tenders in the zone 1 drawer and half in the zone 2 one, then insert the drawers into the unit.
7. Select zone 1, select AIR FRY, set temperature to 390 degrees F/ 200 degrees C, and set time to 10 minutes. Select MATCH to match zone 2 settings to zone 1. Press the START/STOP button to begin cooking.
8. When the time reaches 6 minutes, press START/STOP to pause the unit. Remove the drawers and flip the chicken. Re-insert the drawers into the unit and press START/STOP to resume cooking.
9. When cooking is complete, remove the chicken.

Nutrition Info:

- (Per serving) Calories 244 | Fat 3.6g | Sodium 713mg | Carbs 25.3g | Fiber 0.1g | Sugar 0.1g | Protein 31g

Chicken Parmesan With Roasted Lemon-parmesan Broccoli

Servings:4 | Cooking Time: 18 Minutes

Ingredients:

- FOR THE CHICKEN PARMESAN
- 2 tablespoons all-purpose flour
- 2 large eggs
- 1 cup panko bread crumbs
- 2 tablespoons grated Parmesan cheese
- 2 teaspoons Italian seasoning
- 4 thin-sliced chicken cutlets (4 ounces each)
- 2 tablespoons vegetable oil
- ½ cup marinara sauce
- ½ cup shredded part-skim mozzarella cheese
- FOR THE BROCCOLI
- 4 cups broccoli florets
- 2 tablespoons olive oil, divided
- ¼ teaspoon kosher salt
- ¼ teaspoon freshly ground black pepper
- 2 teaspoons fresh lemon juice
- 2 tablespoons grated Parmesan cheese

Directions:

1. To prep the chicken Parmesan: Set up a breading station with 3 small shallow bowls. Place the flour in the first bowl. In the second bowl, beat the eggs. Combine the panko, Parmesan, and Italian seasoning in the third bowl.
2. Bread the chicken cutlets in this order: First, dip them into the flour, coating both sides. Then, dip into the beaten egg. Finally, place in the panko mixture, coating both sides of the cutlets. Drizzle the oil over the cutlets.
3. To prep the broccoli: In a large bowl, combine the broccoli, 1 tablespoon of olive oil, the salt, and black pepper.
4. To cook the chicken and broccoli: Install a crisper plate in the Zone 1 basket. Place the chicken in the basket and insert the basket in the unit. Place the broccoli in the Zone 2 basket and insert the basket in the unit.
5. Select Zone 1, select AIR FRY, set the temperature to 390°F, and set the time to 18 minutes.
6. Select Zone 2, select ROAST, set the temperature to 390°F, and set the time to 15 minutes. Select SMART FINISH.
7. Press START/PAUSE to begin cooking.
8. When the Zone 1 timer reads 10 minutes, press START/PAUSE. Remove the basket and use silicone-tipped tongs to flip the chicken. Reinsert the basket and press START/PAUSE to resume cooking.
9. When the Zone 1 timer reads 2 minutes, press START/PAUSE. Remove the basket and spoon 2 tablespoons of marinara sauce over each chicken cutlet. Sprinkle the mozzarella on top. Reinsert the basket and press START/PAUSE to resume cooking.
10. When cooking is complete, the cheese will be melted and the chicken cooked through (an instant-read thermometer should read 165°F). Transfer the broccoli to a large bowl. Add the lemon juice and Parmesan and toss to coat. Serve the chicken and broccoli warm.

Nutrition Info:

• (Per serving) Calories: 462; Total fat: 22g; Saturated fat: 5g; Carbohydrates: 25g; Fiber: 2.5g; Protein: 37g; Sodium: 838mg

Pretzel Chicken Cordon Bleu

Servings: 4 | Cooking Time: 26 Minutes

Ingredients:

- 5 boneless chicken thighs
- 3 cups pretzels, crushed
- 2 eggs, beaten
- 10 deli honey ham, slices
- 5 Swiss cheese slices
- Cooking spray

Directions:

1. Grind pretzels in a food processor.
2. Pound the chicken tights with a mallet.
3. Top each chicken piece with one cheese slice and 2 ham slices.
4. Roll the chicken pieces and secure with a toothpick.
5. Dip the rolls in the eggs and coat with the breadcrumbs.
6. Place these rolls in the air fryer baskets.
7. Spray them with cooking oil.
8. Return the air fryer basket 1 to Zone 1, and basket 2 to Zone 2 of the Ninja Foodi 2-Basket Air Fryer.
9. Choose the "Air Fry" mode for Zone 1 and set the temperature to 375 degrees F and 26 minutes of cooking time.
10. Select the "MATCH COOK" option to copy the settings for Zone 2.
11. Initiate cooking by pressing the START/PAUSE BUTTON.
12. Flip the rolls once cooked halfway through.
13. Serve warm.

Nutrition Info:

• (Per serving) Calories 380 | Fat 29g |Sodium 821mg | Carbs 34.6g | Fiber 0g | Sugar 0g | Protein 30g

Chicken Vegetable Skewers

Servings: 6 | Cooking Time: 15 Minutes

Ingredients:

- 900g chicken breasts, cubed
- 1 bell pepper, chopped
- 51g Swerve
- 1 tsp ginger, grated
- 350g zucchini, chopped
- 8 mushrooms, sliced
- ½ medium onion, chopped
- 6 garlic cloves, crushed
- 120ml soy sauce

Directions:

1. Add chicken and the remaining ingredients to a zip-lock bag. Seal the bag and place it in the refrigerator overnight.
2. Thread the marinated chicken, zucchini, mushrooms, onion, and bell pepper onto the skewers.
3. Insert a crisper plate in the Ninja Foodi air fryer baskets.
4. Place skewers in both baskets.
5. Select zone 1 then select "air fry" mode and set the temperature to 380 degrees F for 15 minutes. Press "match" to match zone 2 settings to zone 1. Press "start/stop" to begin.

Nutrition Info:

• (Per serving) Calories 329 | Fat 11.5g |Sodium 1335mg | Carbs 8.6g | Fiber 1.4g | Sugar 2.9g | Protein 46.8g

Thai Curry Chicken Kabobs

Servings: 4 | Cooking Time: 15 Minutes

Ingredients:

- 900g skinless chicken thighs
- 120ml Tamari
- 60ml coconut milk
- 3 tablespoons lime juice
- 3 tablespoons maple syrup
- 2 tablespoons Thai red curry

Directions:

1. Mix red curry paste, honey, lime juice, coconut milk, soy sauce in a bowl.
2. Add this sauce and chicken to a Ziplock bag.
3. Seal the bag and shake it to coat well.
4. Refrigerate the chicken for 2 hours then thread the chicken over wooden skewers.
5. Divide the skewers in the air fryer baskets.
6. Return the air fryer basket 1 to Zone 1, and basket 2 to Zone 2 of the Ninja Foodi 2-Basket Air Fryer.
7. Choose the "Air Fry" mode for Zone 1 at 350 degrees F and 15 minutes of cooking time.
8. Select the "MATCH COOK" option to copy the settings for Zone 2.
9. Initiate cooking by pressing the START/PAUSE BUTTON.
10. Flip the skewers once cooked halfway through.
11. Serve warm.

Nutrition Info:

• (Per serving) Calories 353 | Fat 5g |Sodium 818mg | Carbs 53.2g | Fiber 4.4g | Sugar 8g | Protein 17.3g

Coconut Chicken Tenders With Broiled Utica Greens

Servings:4 | Cooking Time: 25 Minutes

Ingredients:

- FOR THE CHICKEN TENDERS
- 2 tablespoons all-purpose flour
- 2 large eggs
- 1 cup unsweetened shredded coconut
- ¾ cup panko bread crumbs
- ½ teaspoon kosher salt
- 1½ pounds chicken tenders
- Nonstick cooking spray
- FOR THE UTICA GREENS
- 12 ounces frozen chopped escarole or Swiss chard, thawed and drained
- ¼ cup diced prosciutto
- 2 tablespoons chopped pickled cherry peppers
- ½ teaspoon garlic powder
- ½ teaspoon onion powder
- ¼ teaspoon kosher salt
- ¼ cup Italian-style bread crumbs
- ¼ cup grated Romano cheese
- Nonstick cooking spray

Directions:

1. To prep the chicken tenders: Set up a breading station with three small shallow bowls. Place the flour in the first bowl. In the second bowl, beat the eggs. Combine the coconut, bread crumbs, and salt in the third bowl.
2. Bread the chicken tenders in this order: First, coat them in the flour. Then, dip into the beaten egg. Finally, coat them in the coconut breading, gently pressing the breading into the chicken to help it adhere. Mist both sides of each tender with cooking spray.
3. To prep the Utica greens: In the Zone 2 basket, mix the greens, prosciutto, cherry peppers, garlic powder, onion powder, and salt. Scatter the bread crumbs and Romano cheese over the top. Spritz the greens with cooking spray.
4. To cook the chicken and greens: Install a crisper plate in the Zone 1 basket. Place the chicken tenders in the basket in a single layer and insert the basket in the unit. Insert the Zone 2 basket in the unit.
5. Select Zone 1, select AIR FRY, set the temperature to 390°F, and set the time to 25 minutes.
6. Select Zone 2, select AIR BROIL, set the temperature to 450°F, and set the time to 10 minutes. Select SMART FINISH.
7. Press START/PAUSE to begin cooking.
8. When cooking is complete, the chicken will be crispy and cooked through (an instant-read thermometer should read 165°F) and the greens should be warmed through and toasted on top. Serve warm.

Nutrition Info:

- (Per serving) Calories: 527; Total fat: 26g; Saturated fat: 11g; Carbohydrates: 24g; Fiber: 6.5g; Protein: 50g; Sodium: 886mg

Cornish Hen With Asparagus

Servings:2 | Cooking Time:45

Ingredients:

- 10 spears of asparagus
- Salt and black pepper, to taste
- 1 Cornish hen
- Salt, to taste
- Black pepper, to taste
- 1 teaspoon of Paprika
- Coconut spray, for greasing
- 2 lemons, sliced

Directions:

1. Wash and pat dry the asparagus and coat it with coconut oil spray.
2. Sprinkle salt on the asparagus and place inside the first basket of the air fryer.
3. Next, take the Cornish hen and rub it well with the salt, black pepper, and paprika.
4. Oil sprays the Cornish hen and place in the second air fryer basket.
5. Press button 1 for the first basket and set it to AIR FRY mode at 350 degrees F, for 8 minutes.
6. For the second basket hit 2 and set the time to 45 minutes at 350 degrees F, by selecting the ROAST mode.
7. To start cooking, hit the smart finish button and press hit start.
8. Once the 6 minutes pass press 1 and pause and take out the asparagus.
9. Once the chicken cooking cycle complete, press 2 and hit pause.
10. Take out the Basket of chicken and let it transfer to the serving plate
11. Serve the chicken with roasted asparagus and slices of lemon.
12. Serve hot and enjoy.

Nutrition Info:

- (Per serving) Calories 192| Fat 4.7g| Sodium 151mg | Carbs10.7 g | Fiber 4.6g | Sugar 3.8g | Protein 30g

Spice-rubbed Chicken Pieces

Servings:6 | Cooking Time:40

Ingredients:

- 3 pounds chicken, pieces
- 1 teaspoon sweet paprika
- 1 teaspoon mustard powder
- 1 tablespoon brown sugar, dark
- Salt and black pepper, to taste
- 1 teaspoon Chile powder, New Mexico
- 1 teaspoon oregano, dried
- ¼ teaspoon allspice powder, ground

Directions:

1. Take a bowl and mix dark brown sugar, salt, paprika, mustard powder, oregano, Chile powder, black pepper, and all spice powder.
2. Mix well and rub this spice mixture all over the chicken.
3. Divide the chicken between two air fryer baskets.
4. Oil sprays the meat and then adds it to the air fryer.
5. Now press button1 and button 2 and set the time to 40 minutes at 350 degrees F.
6. Now press start and once the cooking cycle completes, press pause for both the zones.
7. Take out the chicken and serve hot.

Nutrition Info:

- (Per serving) Calories353 | Fat 7.1g| Sodium400 mg | Carbs 2.2g | Fibero.4 g | Sugar 1.6g | Protein66 g

Chicken & Broccoli

Servings: 4 | Cooking Time: 20 Minutes

Ingredients:

- 450g chicken breasts, boneless & cut into 1-inch pieces
- 1 tsp sesame oil
- 15ml soy sauce
- 1 tsp garlic powder
- 45ml olive oil
- 350g broccoli florets
- 2 tsp hot sauce
- 2 tsp rice vinegar
- Pepper
- Salt

Directions:

1. In a bowl, add chicken, broccoli florets, and remaining ingredients and mix well.
2. Insert a crisper plate in the Ninja Foodi air fryer baskets.
3. Add the chicken and broccoli mixture in both baskets.
4. Select zone 1, then select "air fry" mode and set the temperature to 380 degrees F for 20 minutes. Press "match" and press"start/stop" to begin.

Nutrition Info:

- (Per serving) Calories 337 | Fat 20.2g |Sodium 440mg | Carbs 3.9g | Fiber 1.3g | Sugar 1g | Protein 34.5g

Chicken Tenders And Curly Fries

Servings: 4 | Cooking Time: 35 Minutes

Ingredients:

- 1-pound frozen chicken tenders
- 1-pound frozen curly French fries
- Dipping sauces of your choice

Directions:

1. Place a crisper plate in each drawer. In the zone 1 drawer, place the chicken tenders, then place the drawer into the unit.
2. Fill the zone 2 drawer with the curly French fries, then place the drawer in the unit.
3. Select zone 1, then AIR FRY, and set the temperature to 390 degrees F/ 200 degrees C with a 22-minute timer. Select zone 2, then AIR FRY, and set the temperature to 400 degrees F/ 200 degrees C with a 30-minute timer. Select SYNC. To begin cooking, press the START/STOP button.
4. Press START/STOP to pause the device when the zone 1 and 2 times reach 8 minutes. Shake the drawers for 10 seconds after removing them from the unit. To resume cooking, re-insert the drawers into the unit and press START/STOP.
5. Enjoy!

Nutrition Info:

- (Per serving) Calories 500 | Fat 19.8g | Sodium 680mg | Carbs 50.1g | Fiber 4.1g | Sugar 0g | Protein 27.9g

Spicy Chicken

Servings:40 | Cooking Time:35

Ingredients:

- 4 chicken thighs
- 2 cups of butter milk
- 4 chicken legs
- 2 cups of flour
- Salt and black pepper, to taste
- 2 tablespoons garlic powder
- ½ teaspoon onion powder
- 1 teaspoon poultry seasoning
- 1 teaspoon cumin
- 2 tablespoons paprika
- 1 tablespoon olive oil

Directions:

1. Take a bowl and add buttermilk to it.
2. Soak the chicken thighs and chicken legs in the buttermilk for 2 hours.
3. Mix flour, all the seasonings, and olive oil in a small bowl.
4. Take out the chicken pieces from the buttermilk mixture and then dredge them into the flour mixture.
5. Repeat the steps for all the pieces and then arrange them into both the air fryer basket.
6. Set the timer for both the basket by selecting a roast mode for 35-40 minutes at 350 degrees F.
7. Once the cooking cycle complete select the pause button and then take out the basket.
8. Serve and enjoy.

Nutrition Info:

- (Per serving) Calories 624| Fat17.6 g| Sodium300 mg | Carbs 60g | Fiber 3.5g | Sugar 7.7g | Protein54.2 g

Honey Butter Chicken

Servings: 4 | Cooking Time: 15 Minutes

Ingredients:

- 4 chicken breasts, boneless
- 85g honey
- 28g butter, melted
- 2 tsp lemon juice
- 15ml olive oil
- 62g Dijon mustard
- Pepper
- Salt

Directions:

1. In a small bowl, mix butter, oil, lemon juice, honey, mustard, pepper, and salt.
2. Insert a crisper plate in the Ninja Foodi air fryer baskets.
3. Brush chicken breasts with butter mixture and place them in both baskets.
4. Select zone 1 then select "bake" mode and set the temperature to 380 degrees F for 15 minutes. Press "match" to match zone 2 settings to zone 1. Press "start/stop" to begin.

Nutrition Info:

- (Per serving) Calories 434 | Fat 20.7g |Sodium 384mg | Carbs 18.4g | Fiber 0.6g | Sugar 17.6g | Protein 43.1g

Crispy Sesame Chicken

Servings: 2 | Cooking Time: 10 Minutes

Ingredients:

- 680g boneless chicken thighs, diced
- 2 tablespoons rice vinegar
- 1 tablespoon soy sauce
- 2 teaspoons minced fresh ginger
- 1 garlic clove, minced
- ¾ teaspoon salt
- ½ teaspoon black pepper
- 2 large eggs, beaten
- 1 cup cornstarch
- Sauce
- 59ml soy sauce
- 2 tablespoons rice vinegar
- ⅓ cup brown sugar
- 59ml water
- 1 tablespoon cornstarch
- 2 teaspoons sesame oil
- 2 tablespoons vegetable oil
- 2 garlic cloves, minced
- 2 teaspoons chile paste
- Garnish
- 1 tablespoon toasted sesame seeds

Directions:

1. Blend all the sauce ingredients in a saucepan and cook until it thickens then allow it to cool.
2. Mix chicken with black pepper, salt, garlic, ginger, vinegar, and soy sauce in a bowl.
3. Cover and marinate the chicken for 20 minutes.
4. Divide the chicken in the air fryer baskets.
5. Return the air fryer basket 1 to Zone 1, and basket 2 to Zone 2 of the Ninja Foodi 2-Basket Air Fryer.
6. Choose the "Air Fry" mode for Zone 1 and set the temperature to 400 degrees F and 10 minutes of cooking time.
7. Select the "MATCH COOK" option to copy the settings for Zone 2.
8. Initiate cooking by pressing the START/PAUSE BUTTON.
9. Pour the prepared sauce over the air fried chicken and drizzle sesame seeds on top.
10. Serve warm.

Nutrition Info:

- (Per serving) Calories 351 | Fat 16g |Sodium 777mg | Carbs 26g | Fiber 4g | Sugar 5g | Protein 28g

Ranch Turkey Tenders With Roasted Vegetable Salad

Servings:4 | Cooking Time: 20 Minutes

Ingredients:

- FOR THE TURKEY TENDERS
- 1 pound turkey tenderloin
- ¼ cup ranch dressing
- ½ cup panko bread crumbs
- Nonstick cooking spray
- FOR THE VEGETABLE SALAD
- 1 large sweet potato, peeled and diced
- 1 zucchini, diced
- 1 red bell pepper, diced
- 1 small red onion, sliced
- 1 tablespoon vegetable oil
- ¼ teaspoon kosher salt
- ½ teaspoon freshly ground black pepper
- 2 cups baby spinach
- ½ cup store-bought balsamic vinaigrette
- ¼ cup chopped walnuts

Directions:

1. To prep the turkey tenders: Slice the turkey crosswise into 16 strips. Brush both sides of each strip with ranch dressing, then coat with the panko. Press the bread crumbs into the turkey to help them adhere. Mist both sides of the strips with cooking spray.
2. To prep the vegetables: In a large bowl, combine the sweet potato, zucchini, bell pepper, onion, and vegetable oil. Stir well to coat the vegetables. Season with the salt and black pepper.
3. To cook the turkey and vegetables: Install a crisper plate in the Zone 1 basket. Place the turkey tenders in the basket in a single layer and insert the basket in the unit. Place the vegetables in the Zone 2 basket and insert the basket in the unit.
4. Select Zone 1, select AIR FRY, set the temperature to 375°F, and set the time to 20 minutes.
5. Select Zone 2, select ROAST, set the temperature to 400°F, and set the time to 20 minutes. Select SMART FINISH.
6. Press START/PAUSE to begin cooking.
7. When both timers read 10 minutes, press START/PAUSE. Remove the Zone 1 basket and use silicone-tipped tongs to flip the turkey tenders. Reinsert the basket in the unit. Remove the Zone 2 basket and shake to redistribute the vegetables. Reinsert the basket and press START/PAUSE to resume cooking.
8. When cooking is complete, the turkey will be golden brown and cooked through (an instant-read thermometer should read 165°F) and the vegetables will be fork-tender.
9. Place the spinach in a large serving bowl. Mix in the roasted vegetables and balsamic vinaigrette. Sprinkle with walnuts. Serve warm with the turkey tenders.

Nutrition Info:

- (Per serving) Calories: 470; Total fat: 28g; Saturated fat: 2.5g; Carbohydrates: 28g; Fiber: 4g; Protein: 31g; Sodium: 718mg

Chicken Bites

Servings: 4 | Cooking Time: 20 Minutes

Ingredients:

- 900g chicken thighs, cut into chunks
- ¼ tsp white pepper
- ½ tsp onion powder
- 30ml olive oil
- 59ml fresh lemon juice
- ½ tsp garlic powder
- Pepper
- Salt

Directions:

1. Add chicken chunks and remaining ingredients into the bowl and mix well.
2. Cover the bowl and place it in the refrigerator overnight.
3. Insert a crisper plate in the Ninja Foodi air fryer baskets.
4. Place the marinated chicken in both baskets.
5. Select zone 1 then select "air fry" mode and set the temperature to 380 degrees F for 20 minutes. Press "match" to match zone 2 settings to zone 1. Press "start/stop" to begin.

Nutrition Info:

- (Per serving) Calories 497 | Fat 23.9g |Sodium 237mg | Carbs 0.9g | Fiber 0.2g | Sugar 0.5g | Protein 65.8g

Almond Chicken

Servings: 4 | Cooking Time: 25 Minutes

Ingredients:

- 2 large eggs
- ½ cup buttermilk
- 2 teaspoons garlic salt
- 1 teaspoon pepper
- 2 cups slivered almonds, finely chopped
- 4 boneless, skinless chicken breast halves (6 ounces each)

Directions:

1. Whisk together the egg, buttermilk, garlic salt, and pepper in a small bowl.
2. In another small bowl, place the almonds.
3. Dip the chicken in the egg mixture, then roll it in the almonds, patting it down to help the coating stick.
4. Install a crisper plate in both drawers. Place half the chicken breasts in the zone 1 drawer and half in zone 2's, then insert the drawers into the unit.
5. Select zone 1, select AIR FRY, set temperature to 390 degrees F/ 200 degrees C, and set time to 22 minutes. Select MATCH to match zone 2 settings to zone 1. Press the START/STOP button to begin cooking.
6. When the time reaches 11 minutes, press START/STOP to pause the unit. Remove the drawers and flip the chicken. Re-insert the drawers into the unit and press START/STOP to resume cooking.
7. When cooking is complete, remove the chicken.

Nutrition Info:

- (Per serving) Calories 353 | Fat 18g | Sodium 230mg | Carbs 6g | Fiber 2g | Sugar 3g | Protein 41g

VEGETABLES AND SIDES RECIPES

Vegetables And Sides Recipes

Breaded Summer Squash

Servings: 4 | Cooking Time: 10 Minutes

Ingredients:

- 4 cups yellow summer squash, sliced
- 3 tablespoons olive oil
- ½ teaspoon salt
- ½ teaspoon pepper
- ⅛ teaspoon cayenne pepper
- ¾ cup panko bread crumbs
- ¾ cup grated Parmesan cheese

Directions:

1. Mix crumbs, cheese, cayenne pepper, black pepper, salt and oil in a bowl.
2. Coat the squash slices with the breadcrumb mixture.
3. Place these slices in the air fryer baskets.
4. Return the air fryer basket 1 to Zone 1, and basket 2 to Zone 2 of the Ninja Foodi 2-Basket Air Fryer.
5. Choose the "Air Fry" mode for Zone 1 at 350 degrees F and 10 minutes of cooking time.
6. Select the "MATCH COOK" option to copy the settings for Zone 2.
7. Initiate cooking by pressing the START/PAUSE BUTTON.
8. Flip the squash slices once cooked half way through.
9. Serve warm.

Nutrition Info:

- (Per serving) Calories 193 | Fat 1g |Sodium 395mg | Carbs 38.7g | Fiber 1.6g | Sugar 0.9g | Protein 6.6g

Healthy Air Fried Veggies

Servings: 4 | Cooking Time: 15 Minutes

Ingredients:

- 52g onion, sliced
- 71g broccoli florets
- 116g radishes, sliced
- 15ml olive oil
- 100g Brussels sprouts, cut in half
- 325g cauliflower florets
- 1 tsp balsamic vinegar
- ½ tsp garlic powder
- Pepper
- Salt

Directions:

1. In a bowl, toss veggies with oil, vinegar, garlic powder, pepper, and salt.
2. Insert a crisper plate in the Ninja Foodi air fryer baskets.
3. Add veggies in both baskets.
4. Select zone 1 then select "air fry" mode and set the temperature to 380 degrees F for 15 minutes. Press "match" to match zone 2 settings to zone 1. Press "start/stop" to begin. Stir halfway through.

Nutrition Info:

- (Per serving) Calories 71 | Fat 3.8g |Sodium 72mg | Carbs 8.8g | Fiber 3.2g | Sugar 3.3g | Protein 2.5g

Air-fried Radishes

Servings: 6 | Cooking Time: 15 Minutes

Ingredients:

- 1020g radishes, quartered
- 3 tablespoons olive oil
- 1 tablespoon fresh oregano, minced
- ¼ teaspoon salt
- ⅛ teaspoon black pepper

Directions:

1. Toss radishes with oil, black pepper, salt and oregano in a bowl.
2. Divide the radishes into the Ninja Foodi 2 Baskets Air Fryer baskets.
3. Return the air fryer basket 1 to Zone 1, and basket 2 to Zone 2 of the Ninja Foodi 2-Basket Air Fryer.
4. Choose the "Air Fry" mode for Zone 1 at 375 degrees F and 15 minutes of cooking time.
5. Select the "MATCH COOK" option to copy the settings for Zone 2.
6. Initiate cooking by pressing the START/PAUSE BUTTON.
7. Toss the radishes once cooked halfway through.
8. Serve.

Nutrition Info:

- (Per serving) Calories 270 | Fat 14.6g |Sodium 394mg | Carbs 31.3g | Fiber 7.5g | Sugar 9.7g | Protein 6.4g

Buffalo Seitan With Crispy Zucchini Noodles

Servings:4 | Cooking Time: 12 Minutes

Ingredients:

- FOR THE BUFFALO SEITAN
- 1 (8-ounce) package precooked seitan strips
- 1 teaspoon garlic powder, divided
- ½ teaspoon onion powder
- ¼ teaspoon smoked paprika
- ¼ cup Louisiana-style hot sauce
- 2 tablespoons vegetable oil
- 1 tablespoon tomato paste
- ¼ teaspoon freshly ground black pepper
- FOR THE ZUCCHINI NOODLES
- 3 large egg whites
- 1¼ cups all-purpose flour
- 1 teaspoon kosher salt, divided
- 12 ounces seltzer water or club soda
- 5 ounces zucchini noodles
- Nonstick cooking spray

Directions:

1. To prep the Buffalo seitan: Season the seitan strips with ½ teaspoon of garlic powder, the onion powder, and smoked paprika.
2. In a large bowl, whisk together the hot sauce, oil, tomato paste, remaining ½ teaspoon of garlic powder, and the black pepper. Set the bowl of Buffalo sauce aside.
3. To prep the zucchini noodles: In a medium bowl, use a handheld mixer to beat the egg whites until stiff peaks form.
4. In a large bowl, combine the flour and ½ teaspoon of salt. Mix in the seltzer to form a thin batter. Fold in the beaten egg whites.
5. Add the zucchini to the batter and gently mix to coat.
6. To cook the seitan and zucchini noodles: Install a crisper plate in each of the two baskets. Place the seitan in the Zone 1 basket and insert the basket in the unit. Lift the noodles from the batter one at a time, letting the excess drip off, and place them in the Zone 2 basket. Insert the basket in the unit.
7. Select Zone 1, select BAKE, set the temperature to 370°F, and set the timer to 12 minutes.
8. Select Zone 2, select AIR FRY, set the temperature to 400°F, and set the timer to 12 minutes. Select SMART FINISH.
9. Press START/PAUSE to begin cooking.
10. When the Zone 1 timer reads 2 minutes, press START/PAUSE. Remove the basket and transfer the seitan to the bowl of Buffalo sauce. Turn to coat, then return the seitan to the basket. Reinsert the basket and press START/PAUSE to resume cooking.
11. When cooking is complete, the seitan should be warmed through and the zucchini noodles crisp and light golden brown.
12. Sprinkle the zucchini noodles with the remaining ½ teaspoon of salt. If desired, drizzle extra Buffalo sauce over the seitan. Serve hot.

Nutrition Info:

- (Per serving) Calories: 252; Total fat: 15g; Saturated fat: 1g; Carbohydrates: 22g; Fiber: 1.5g; Protein: 13g; Sodium: 740mg

Potatoes & Beans

Servings: 4 | Cooking Time: 25 Minutes

Ingredients:

- 453g potatoes, cut into pieces
- 15ml olive oil
- 1 tsp garlic powder
- 160g green beans, trimmed
- Pepper
- Salt

Directions:

1. In a bowl, toss green beans, garlic powder, potatoes, oil, pepper, and salt.
2. Insert a crisper plate in the Ninja Foodi air fryer baskets.
3. Add green beans and potato mixture to both baskets.
4. Select zone 1 then select "air fry" mode and set the temperature to 380 degrees F for 25 minutes. Press "match" to match zone 2 settings to zone 1. Press "start/stop" to begin. Stir halfway through.

Nutrition Info:

- (Per serving) Calories 128 | Fat 3.7g |Sodium 49mg | Carbs 22.4g | Fiber 4.7g | Sugar 2.3g | Protein 3.1g

Garlic-rosemary Brussels Sprouts

Servings: 4 | Cooking Time: 8 Minutes

Ingredients:

- 3 tablespoons olive oil
- 2 garlic cloves, minced
- ½ teaspoon salt
- ¼ teaspoon black pepper
- 455g Brussels sprouts, halved
- ½ cup panko bread crumbs
- 1-½ teaspoons rosemary, minced

Directions:

1. Toss the Brussels sprouts with crumbs and the rest of the ingredients in a bowl.
2. Divide the sprouts into the Ninja Foodi 2 Baskets Air Fryer baskets.
3. Return the air fryer basket 1 to Zone 1, and basket 2 to Zone 2 of the Ninja Foodi 2-Basket Air Fryer.
4. Choose the "Air Fry" mode for Zone 1 at 350 degrees F and 8 minutes of cooking time.
5. Select the "MATCH COOK" option to copy the settings for Zone 2.
6. Initiate cooking by pressing the START/PAUSE BUTTON.
7. Toss the Brussels sprouts once cooked halfway through.
8. Serve warm.

Nutrition Info:

- (Per serving) Calories 231 | Fat 9g |Sodium 271mg | Carbs 32.8g | Fiber 6.4g | Sugar 7g | Protein 6.3g

Fried Patty Pan Squash

Servings: 6 | Cooking Time: 15 Minutes

Ingredients:

- 5 cups small pattypan squash, halved
- 1 tablespoon olive oil
- 2 garlic cloves, minced
- ½ teaspoon salt
- ¼ teaspoon dried oregano
- ¼ teaspoon dried thyme
- ¼ teaspoon pepper
- 1 tablespoon minced parsley

Directions:

1. Rub the squash with oil, garlic and the rest of the ingredients.
2. Spread the squash in the air fryer baskets.
3. Return the air fryer basket 1 to Zone 1, and basket 2 to Zone 2 of the Ninja Foodi 2-Basket Air Fryer.
4. Choose the "Air Fry" mode for Zone 1 at 375 degrees F and 15 minutes of cooking time.
5. Select the "MATCH COOK" option to copy the settings for Zone 2.
6. Initiate cooking by pressing the START/PAUSE BUTTON.
7. Flip the squash once cooked halfway through.
8. Garnish with parsley.
9. Serve warm.

Nutrition Info:

- (Per serving) Calories 208 | Fat 5g |Sodium 1205mg | Carbs 34.1g | Fiber 7.8g | Sugar 2.5g | Protein 5.9g

Saucy Carrots

Servings: 6 | Cooking Time: 25 Minutes.

Ingredients:

- 1 lb. cup carrots, cut into chunks
- 1 tablespoon sesame oil
- ½ tablespoon ginger, minced
- ½ tablespoon soy sauce
- ½ teaspoon garlic, minced
- ½ tablespoon scallions, chopped, for garnish
- ½ teaspoon sesame seeds for garnish

Directions:

1. Toss all the ginger carrots ingredients, except the sesame seeds and scallions, in a suitable bowl.
2. Divide the carrots in the two crisper plates in a single layer.
3. Return the crisper plates to the Ninja Foodi Dual Zone Air Fryer.
4. Choose the Air Fry mode for Zone 1 and set the temperature to 390 degrees F and the time to 25 minutes.
5. Select the "MATCH" button to copy the settings for Zone 2.
6. Initiate cooking by pressing the START/STOP button.
7. Toss the carrots once cooked halfway through.
8. Garnish with sesame seeds and scallions.
9. Serve warm.

Nutrition Info:

- (Per serving) Calories 206 | Fat 3.4g |Sodium 174mg | Carbs 35g | Fiber 9.4g | Sugar 5.9g | Protein 10.6g

Potato And Parsnip Latkes With Baked Apples

Servings:4 | Cooking Time: 20 Minutes

Ingredients:

- FOR THE LATKES
- 2 medium russet potatoes, peeled
- 1 large egg white
- 2 tablespoons all-purpose flour
- ¼ teaspoon garlic powder
- ¼ teaspoon kosher salt
- ¼ teaspoon freshly ground black pepper
- 1 medium parsnip, peeled and shredded
- 2 scallions, thinly sliced
- 2 tablespoons vegetable oil
- FOR THE BAKED APPLES
- 2 Golden Delicious apples, peeled and diced
- 2 tablespoons granulated sugar

- 2 teaspoons unsalted butter, cut into small pieces

Directions:

1. To prep the latkes: Grate the potatoes using the large holes of a box grater. Squeeze as much liquid out of the potatoes as you can into a large bowl. Set the potatoes aside in a separate bowl.
2. Let the potato liquid sit for 5 minutes, during which time the potato starch will settle to the bottom of the bowl. Pour off the water that has risen to the top, leaving the potato starch in the bowl.
3. Add the egg white, flour, salt, and black pepper to the potato starch to form a thick paste. Add the potatoes, parsnip, and scallions and mix well. Divide the mixture into 4 patties. Brush both sides of each patty with the oil.
4. To prep the baked apples: Place the apples in the Zone 2 basket. Sprinkle the sugar and butter over the top.
5. To cook the latkes and apples: Install a crisper plate in the Zone 1 basket. Place the latkes in the basket in a single layer, then insert the basket in the unit. Insert the Zone 2 basket in the unit.
6. Select Zone 1, select AIR FRY, set the temperature to 375°F, and set the timer to 15 minutes.
7. Select Zone 2, select BAKE, set the temperature to 330°F, and set the timer to 20 minutes. Select SMART FINISH.
8. Press START/PAUSE to begin cooking.
9. When both timers read 5 minutes, press START/PAUSE. Remove the Zone 1 basket and use silicone-tipped tongs or a spatula to flip the latkes. Reinsert the basket in the unit. Remove the Zone 2 basket and gently mash the apples with a fork or the back of a spoon. Reinsert the basket and press START/PAUSE to resume cooking.
10. When cooking is complete, the latkes should be golden brown and cooked through and the apples very soft.
11. Transfer the latkes to a plate and serve with apples on the side.

Nutrition Info:

- (Per serving) Calories: 257; Total fat: 9g; Saturated fat: 2g; Carbohydrates: 42g; Fiber: 5.5g; Protein: 4g; Sodium: 91mg

Green Beans With Baked Potatoes

Servings:2 | Cooking Time:45

Ingredients:

- 2 cups of green beans
- 2 large potatoes, cubed
- 3 tablespoons of olive oil
- 1 teaspoon of seasoned salt
- ½ teaspoon chili powder
- 1/6 teaspoon garlic powder
- 1/4 teaspoon onion powder

Directions:

1. Take a large bowl and pour olive oil into it.
2. Now add all the seasoning in the olive oil and whisk it well.
3. Toss the green bean in it, then transfer it to zone 1 basket of the air fryer.
4. Now season the potatoes with the seasoning and add them to the zone 2 basket.
5. Now set the zone one basket to AIRFRY mode at 350 degrees F for 18 minutes.
6. Now hit 2 for the second basket and set it to AIR FRY mode at 350 degrees F, for 45 minutes.
7. Once the cooking cycle is complete, take out and serve it by transferring it to the serving plates.

Nutrition Info:

- (Per serving) Calories473 | Fat21.6g | Sodium796 mg | Carbs 66.6g | Fiber12.9 g | Sugar6 g | Protein8.4 g

Green Tomato Stacks

Servings: 6 | Cooking Time: 12 Minutes

Ingredients:

- ¼ cup mayonnaise
- ¼ teaspoon lime zest, grated
- 2 tablespoons lime juice
- 1 teaspoon minced fresh thyme
- ½ teaspoon black pepper
- ¼ cup all-purpose flour
- 2 large egg whites, beaten
- ¾ cup cornmeal
- ¼ teaspoon salt
- 2 medium green tomatoes
- 2 medium re tomatoes
- Cooking spray
- 8 slices Canadian bacon, warmed

Directions:

1. Mix mayonnaise with ¼ teaspoon black pepper, thyme, lime juice and zest in a bowl.
2. Spread flour in one bowl, beat egg whites in another bowl and mix cornmeal with ¼ teaspoon black pepper and salt in a third bowl.
3. Cut the tomatoes into 4 slices and coat each with the flour then dip in the egg whites.
4. Coat the tomatoes slices with the cornmeal mixture.

5. Place the slices in the air fryer baskets.
6. Return the air fryer basket 1 to Zone 1, and basket 2 to Zone 2 of the Ninja Foodi 2-Basket Air Fryer.
7. Choose the "Air Fry" mode for Zone 1 at 390 degrees F and 12 minutes of cooking time.
8. Select the "MATCH COOK" option to copy the settings for Zone 2.
9. Initiate cooking by pressing the START/PAUSE BUTTON.
10. Flip the tomatoes once cooked halfway through.
11. Place the green tomato slices on the working surface.
12. Top them with bacon, and red tomato slice.
13. Serve.

Nutrition Info:

- (Per serving) Calories 113 | Fat 3g |Sodium 152mg | Carbs 20g | Fiber 3g | Sugar 1.1g | Protein 3.5g

Flavourful Mexican Cauliflower

Servings: 4 | Cooking Time: 12 Minutes

Ingredients:

- 1 medium cauliflower head, cut into florets
- ½ tsp turmeric
- 1 tsp onion powder
- 2 tsp garlic powder
- 2 tsp parsley
- 1 lime juice
- 30ml olive oil
- 1 tsp chilli powder
- 1 tsp cumin
- Pepper
- Salt

Directions:

1. In a bowl, toss cauliflower florets with onion powder, garlic powder, parsley, oil, chilli powder, turmeric, cumin, pepper, and salt.
2. Insert a crisper plate in the Ninja Foodi air fryer baskets.
3. Add cauliflower florets in both baskets.
4. Select zone 1, then select "air fry" mode and set the temperature to 390 degrees F for 12 minutes. Press "match" to match zone 2 settings to zone 1. Press "start/stop" to begin. Stir halfway through.
5. Drizzle lime juice over cauliflower florets.

Nutrition Info:

- (Per serving) Calories 108 | Fat 7.4g |Sodium 91mg | Carbs 10g | Fiber 4.1g | Sugar 4.1g | Protein 3.4g

Chickpea Fritters

Servings: 6 | Cooking Time: 6 Minutes

Ingredients:

- 237ml plain yogurt
- 2 tablespoons sugar
- 1 tablespoon honey
- ½ teaspoon salt
- ½ teaspoon black pepper
- ½ teaspoon crushed red pepper flakes
- 1 can (28g) chickpeas, drained
- 1 teaspoon ground cumin
- ½ teaspoon salt
- ½ teaspoon garlic powder
- ½ teaspoon ground ginger
- 1 large egg
- ½ teaspoon baking soda
- ½ cup fresh coriander, chopped
- 2 green onions, sliced

Directions:

1. Mash chickpeas with rest of the ingredients in a food processor.
2. Layer the two air fryer baskets with a parchment paper.
3. Drop the batter in the baskets spoon by spoon.
4. Return the air fryer basket 1 to Zone 1, and basket 2 to Zone 2 of the Ninja Foodi 2-Basket Air Fryer.
5. Choose the "Air Fry" mode for Zone 1 at 400 degrees F and 6 minutes of cooking time.
6. Select the "MATCH COOK" option to copy the settings for Zone 2.
7. Initiate cooking by pressing the START/PAUSE BUTTON.
8. Flip the fritters once cooked halfway through.
9. Serve warm.

Nutrition Info:

- (Per serving) Calories 284 | Fat 7.9g |Sodium 704mg | Carbs 38.1g | Fiber 1.9g | Sugar 1.9g | Protein 14.8g

Balsamic Vegetables

Servings: 4 | Cooking Time: 13 Minutes

Ingredients:

- 125g asparagus, cut woody ends
- 88g mushrooms, halved
- 1 tbsp Dijon mustard
- 3 tbsp soy sauce
- 27g brown sugar
- 57ml balsamic vinegar
- 32g olive oil
- 1 zucchini, sliced
- 1 yellow squash, sliced
- 170g grape tomatoes
- Pepper
- Salt

Directions:

1. In a bowl, mix asparagus, tomatoes, oil, mustard, soy sauce, mushrooms, zucchini, squash, brown sugar, vinegar, pepper, and salt.
2. Cover the bowl and place it in the refrigerator for 45 minutes.
3. Insert a crisper plate in the Ninja Foodi air fryer baskets.

4. Add the vegetable mixture in both baskets.
5. Select zone 1, then select "air fry" mode and set the temperature to 390 degrees F for 12 minutes. Press "match" to match zone 2 settings to zone 1. Press "start/stop" to begin. Stir halfway through.

Nutrition Info:

- (Per serving) Calories 184 | Fat 13.3g |Sodium 778mg | Carbs 14.7g | Fiber 3.6g | Sugar 9.5g | Protein 5.5g

Quinoa Patties

Servings: 4 | Cooking Time: 32 Minutes.

Ingredients:

- 1 cup quinoa red
- 1½ cups water
- 1 teaspoon salt
- black pepper, ground
- 1½ cups rolled oats
- 3 eggs beaten
- ¼ cup minced white onion
- ½ cup crumbled feta cheese
- ¼ cup chopped fresh chives
- Salt and black pepper, to taste
- Vegetable or canola oil
- 4 hamburger buns
- 4 arugulas
- 4 slices tomato sliced
- Cucumber yogurt dill sauce
- 1 cup cucumber, diced
- 1 cup Greek yogurt
- 2 teaspoons lemon juice
- ¼ teaspoon salt
- Black pepper, ground
- 1 tablespoon chopped fresh dill
- 1 tablespoon olive oil

Directions:

1. Add quinoa to a saucepan filled with cold water, salt, and black pepper, and place it over medium-high heat.
2. Cook the quinoa to a boil, then reduce the heat, cover, and cook for 20 minutes on a simmer.
3. Fluff and mix the cooked quinoa with a fork and remove it from the heat.
4. Spread the quinoa in a baking stay.
5. Mix eggs, oats, onion, herbs, cheese, salt, and black pepper.
6. Stir in quinoa, then mix well. Make 4 patties out of this quinoa cheese mixture.
7. Divide the patties in the two crisper plates and spray them with cooking oil.
8. Return the crisper plates to the Ninja Foodi Dual Zone Air Fryer.
9. Choose the Air Fry mode for Zone 1 and set the temperature to 390 degrees F and the time to 13 minutes.
10. Select the "MATCH" button to copy the settings for Zone 2.
11. Initiate cooking by pressing the START/STOP button.
12. Flip the patties once cooked halfway through, and resume cooking.
13. Meanwhile, prepare the cucumber yogurt dill sauce by mixing all of its ingredients in a mixing bowl.
14. Place each quinoa patty in a burger bun along with arugula leaves.
15. Serve with yogurt dill sauce.

Nutrition Info:

- (Per serving) Calories 231 | Fat 9g |Sodium 271mg | Carbs 32.8g | Fiber 6.4g | Sugar 7g | Protein 6.3g

Garlic Herbed Baked Potatoes

Servings:4 | Cooking Time:45

Ingredients:

- 4 large baking potatoes
- Salt and black pepper, to taste
- 2 teaspoons of avocado oil
- Cheese ingredients
- 2 cups sour cream
- 1 teaspoon of garlic clove, minced
- 1 teaspoon fresh dill
- 2 teaspoons chopped chives
- Salt and black pepper, to taste
- 2 teaspoons Worcestershire sauce

Directions:

1. Pierce the skin of potatoes with a fork.
2. Season the potatoes with olive oil, salt, and black pepper.
3. Divide the potatoes among two baskets of the ninja air fryer.
4. Now hit 1 for the first basket and set it to AIR FRY mode at 350 degrees F, for 45 minutes.
5. Select the MATCH button for zone 2.
6. Meanwhile, take a bowl and mix all the ingredient under cheese ingredients
7. Once the cooking cycle complete, take out and make a slit in-between the potatoes.
8. Add cheese mixture in the cavity and serve it hot.

Nutrition Info:

- (Per serving) Calories 382| Fat24.6 g| Sodium 107mg | Carbs 36.2g | Fiber 2.5g | Sugar2 g | Protein 7.3g

Spanakopita Rolls With Mediterranean Vegetable Salad

Servings:4 | Cooking Time: 15 Minutes

Ingredients:

- FOR THE SPANAKOPITA ROLLS
- 1 (10-ounce) package chopped frozen spinach, thawed
- 4 ounces feta cheese, crumbled
- 2 large eggs
- 1 teaspoon dried oregano
- ½ teaspoon freshly ground black pepper
- 12 sheets phyllo dough, thawed
- Nonstick cooking spray
- FOR THE ROASTED VEGETABLES
- 1 medium eggplant, diced
- 1 small red onion, cut into 8 wedges
- 1 red bell pepper, sliced
- 2 tablespoons olive oil
- FOR THE SALAD
- 1 (15-ounce) can chickpeas, drained and rinsed
- ¼ cup chopped fresh parsley
- ¼ cup olive oil
- ¼ cup red wine vinegar
- 2 garlic cloves, minced
- ½ teaspoon dried oregano
- ¼ teaspoon kosher salt
- ¼ teaspoon freshly ground black pepper

Directions:

1. To prep the spanakopita rolls: Squeeze as much liquid from the spinach as you can and place the spinach in a large bowl. Add the feta, eggs, oregano, and black pepper. Mix well.
2. Lay one sheet of phyllo on a clean work surface and mist it with cooking spray. Place another sheet of phyllo directly on top of the first sheet and mist it with cooking spray. Repeat with a third sheet.
3. Spoon one-quarter of the spinach mixture along one short side of the phyllo. Fold the long sides in over the spinach, then roll up it like a burrito.
4. Repeat this process with the remaining phyllo sheets and spinach mixture to form 4 rolls.
5. To prep the vegetables: In a large bowl, combine the eggplant, onion, bell pepper, and oil. Mix well.
6. To cook the rolls and vegetables: Install a crisper plate in each of the two baskets. Place the spanakopita rolls seam-side down in the Zone 1 basket, and spritz the rolls with cooking spray. Place the vegetables in the Zone 2 basket and insert both baskets in the unit.
7. Select Zone 1, select AIR FRY, set the temperature to 375°F, and set the timer to 10 minutes.
8. Select Zone 2, select ROAST, set the temperature to 375°F, and set the timer to 15 minutes. Select SMART FINISH.
9. Press START/PAUSE to begin cooking.
10. When the Zone 1 timer reads 3 minutes, press START/PAUSE. Remove the basket and use silicone-tipped tongs or a spatula to flip the spanakopita rolls. Reinsert the basket and press START/PAUSE to resume cooking.
11. When cooking is complete, the rolls should be crisp and golden brown and the vegetables tender.
12. To assemble the salad: Transfer the roasted vegetables to a large bowl. Stir in the chickpeas and parsley.
13. In a small bowl, whisk together the oil, vinegar, garlic, oregano, salt, and black pepper. Pour the dressing over the vegetables and toss to coat. Serve warm.

Nutrition Info:

- (Per serving) Calories: 739; Total fat: 51g; Saturated fat: 8g; Carbohydrates: 67g; Fiber: 11g; Protein: 21g; Sodium: 806mg

Fried Asparagus

Servings: 4 | Cooking Time: 6 Minutes

Ingredients:

- ¼ cup mayonnaise
- 4 teaspoons olive oil
- 1½ teaspoons grated lemon zest
- 1 garlic clove, minced
- ½ teaspoon pepper
- ¼ teaspoon seasoned salt
- 1-pound fresh asparagus, trimmed
- 2 tablespoons shredded parmesan cheese
- Lemon wedges (optional)

Directions:

1. In a large bowl, combine the first 6 ingredients.
2. Add the asparagus; toss to coat.
3. Put a crisper plate in both drawers. Put the asparagus in a single layer in each drawer. Top with the parmesan cheese. Place the drawers into the unit.
4. Select zone 1, then AIR FRY, then set the temperature to 375 degrees F/ 190 degrees C with a 6-minute timer. To match zone 2 settings to zone 1, choose MATCH. To begin, select START/STOP.
5. Remove the asparagus from the drawers after the timer has finished.

Nutrition Info:

- (Per serving) Calories 156 | Fat 15g | Sodium 214mg | Carbs 3g | Fiber 1g | Sugar 1g | Protein 2g

Brussels Sprouts

Servings:2 | Cooking Time:20

Ingredients:

- 2 pounds Brussels sprouts
- 2 tablespoons avocado oil
- Salt and pepper, to taste
- 1 cup pine nuts, roasted

Directions:

1. Trim the bottom of Brussels sprouts.
2. Take a bowl and combine the avocado oil, salt, and black pepper.
3. Toss the Brussels sprouts well.
4. Divide it in both air fryer baskets.
5. For the zone 1 basket use AIR fry mode for 20 minutes at 390 degrees F.
6. Select the MATCH button for the zone 2 basket.
7. Once the Brussels sprouts get crisp and tender, take out and serve.

Nutrition Info:

- (Per serving) Calories 672| Fat 50g| Sodium 115mg | Carbs 51g | Fiber 20.2g | Sugar 12.3g | Protein 25g

Rosemary Asparagus & Potatoes

Servings: 6 | Cooking Time: 30 Minutes

Ingredients:

- 125g asparagus, trimmed & cut into pieces
- 2 tsp garlic powder
- 2 tbsp rosemary, chopped
- 30ml olive oil
- 679g baby potatoes, quartered
- ½ tsp red pepper flakes
- Pepper
- Salt

Directions:

1. Insert a crisper plate in the Ninja Foodi air fryer baskets.
2. Toss potatoes with 1 tablespoon of oil, pepper, and salt in a bowl until well coated.
3. Add potatoes into in zone 1 basket.
4. Toss asparagus with remaining oil, red pepper flakes, pepper, garlic powder, and rosemary in a mixing bowl.
5. Add asparagus into the zone 2 basket.
6. Select zone 1, then select "air fry" mode and set the temperature to 390 degrees F for 20 minutes. Select zone 2, then select "air fry" mode and set the temperature to 390 degrees F for 10 minutes. Press "match" mode, then press "start/stop" to begin.

Nutrition Info:

- (Per serving) Calories 121 | Fat 5g |Sodium 40mg | Carbs 17.1g | Fiber 4.2g | Sugar 1g | Protein 4g

Mushroom Roll-ups

Servings: 10 | Cooking Time: 11 Minutes.

Ingredients:

- 2 tablespoons olive oil
- 227g portobello mushrooms, chopped
- 1 teaspoon dried oregano
- 1 teaspoon dried thyme
- ½ teaspoon crushed red pepper flakes
- ¼ teaspoon salt
- 1 package (227g) cream cheese, softened
- 113g whole-milk ricotta cheese
- 10 (8 inches) flour tortillas
- Cooking spray
- Chutney

Directions:

1. Sauté mushrooms with oil, thyme, salt, pepper flakes, and oregano in a skillet for 4 minutes.
2. Mix cheeses and add sauteed mushrooms the mix well.
3. Divide the mushroom mixture over the tortillas.
4. Roll the tortillas and secure with a toothpick.
5. Place the rolls in the air fryer basket.
6. Return the air fryer basket 1 to Zone 1, and basket 2 to Zone 2 of the Ninja Foodi 2-Basket Air Fryer.
7. Choose the "Air Fry" mode for Zone 1 and set the temperature to 400 degrees F and 11 minutes of cooking time.
8. Select the "MATCH COOK" option to copy the settings for Zone 2.
9. Initiate cooking by pressing the START/PAUSE BUTTON.
10. Flip the rolls once cooked halfway through.
11. Serve warm.

Nutrition Info:

- (Per serving) Calories 288 | Fat 6.9g |Sodium 761mg | Carbs 46g | Fiber 4g | Sugar 12g | Protein 9.6g

Air Fried Okra

Servings: 2 | Cooking Time: 13 Minutes.

Ingredients:

- ½ lb. okra pods sliced
- 1 teaspoon olive oil
- ¼ teaspoon salt
- ⅛ teaspoon black pepper

Directions:

1. Preheat the Ninja Foodi Dual Zone Air Fryer to 350 degrees F.

2. Toss okra with olive oil, salt, and black pepper in a bowl.
3. Spread the okra in a single layer in the two crisper plates.
4. Return the crisper plate to the Ninja Foodi Dual Zone Air Fryer.
5. Choose the Air Fry mode for Zone 1 and set the temperature to 375 degrees F and the time to 13 minutes.
6. Select the "MATCH" button to copy the settings for Zone 2.
7. Initiate cooking by pressing the START/STOP button.
8. Toss the okra once cooked halfway through, and resume cooking.
9. Serve warm.

Nutrition Info:

- (Per serving) Calories 208 | Fat 5g |Sodium 1205mg | Carbs 34.1g | Fiber 7.8g | Sugar 2.5g | Protein 5.9g

Kale And Spinach Chips

Servings:2 | Cooking Time:6

Ingredients:

- 2 cups spinach, torn in pieces and stem removed
- 2 cups kale, torn in pieces, stems removed
- 1 tablespoon of olive oil
- Sea salt, to taste
- 1/3 cup Parmesan cheese

Directions:

1. Take a bowl and add spinach to it.
2. Take another bowl and add kale to it.
3. Now, season both of them with olive oil, and sea salt.
4. Add kale to zone 1 basket and spinach to zone 2 basket.
5. Select the zone 1 air fry mode at 350 degrees F for 6 minutes.
6. Set zone 2 to AIR FRY mode at 350 for 5 minutes.
7. Once done, take out the crispy chips and sprinkle Parmesan cheese on top.
8. Serve and Enjoy.

Nutrition Info:

- (Per serving) Calories 166| Fat 11.1g| Sodium 355mg | Carbs 8.1g | Fiber1.7 g | Sugar 0.1g | Protein 8.2g

Balsamic-glazed Tofu With Roasted Butternut Squash

Servings:4 | Cooking Time: 40 Minutes

Ingredients:

- FOR THE BALSAMIC TOFU
- 2 tablespoons balsamic vinegar
- 1 tablespoon maple syrup
- 1 teaspoon soy sauce
- 1 teaspoon Dijon mustard
- 1 (14-ounce) package firm tofu, drained and cut into large cubes
- 1 tablespoon canola oil
- FOR THE BUTTERNUT SQUASH
- 1 small butternut squash
- 1 tablespoon canola oil
- 1 teaspoon light brown sugar
- ¼ teaspoon kosher salt
- ¼ teaspoon freshly ground black pepper

Directions:

1. To prep the balsamic tofu: In a large bowl, whisk together the vinegar, maple syrup, soy sauce, and mustard. Add the tofu and stir to coat. Cover and marinate for at least 20 minutes (or up to overnight in the refrigerator).
2. To prep the butternut squash: Peel the squash and cut in half lengthwise. Remove and discard the seeds. Cut the squash crosswise into ½-inch-thick slices.
3. Brush the squash pieces with the oil, then sprinkle with the brown sugar, salt, and black pepper.
4. To cook the tofu and squash: Install a crisper plate in each of the two baskets. Place the tofu in the Zone 1 basket, drizzle with the oil, and insert the basket in the unit. Place the squash in the Zone 2 basket and insert the basket in the unit.
5. Select Zone 1, select AIR FRY, set the temperature to 400°F, and set the timer to 10 minutes.
6. Select Zone 2, select ROAST, set the temperature to 400°F, and set the timer to 40 minutes. Select SMART FINISH.
7. Press START/PAUSE to begin cooking.
8. When cooking is complete, the tofu will have begun to crisp and brown around the edges and the squash should be tender. Serve hot.

Nutrition Info:

- (Per serving) Calories: 253; Total fat: 11g; Saturated fat: 1g; Carbohydrates: 30g; Fiber: 4.5g; Protein: 11g; Sodium: 237mg

Lemon Herb Cauliflower

Servings: 4 | Cooking Time: 10 Minutes

Ingredients:

- 384g cauliflower florets
- 1 tsp lemon zest, grated
- 1 tbsp thyme, minced
- 60ml olive oil
- 1 tbsp rosemary, minced
- ¼ tsp red pepper flakes, crushed
- 30ml lemon juice
- 25g parsley, minced
- ½ tsp salt

Directions:

1. In a bowl, toss cauliflower florets with the remaining ingredients until well coated.
2. Insert a crisper plate in the Ninja Foodi air fryer baskets.
3. Add cauliflower florets into both baskets.
4. Select zone 1, then select "air fry" mode and set the temperature to 360 degrees F for 10 minutes. Press "match" and "start/stop" to begin.

Nutrition Info:

- (Per serving) Calories 166 | Fat 14.4g |Sodium 340mg | Carbs 9.5g | Fiber 4.6g | Sugar 3.8g | Protein 3.3g

Jerk Tofu With Roasted Cabbage

Servings:4 | Cooking Time: 20 Minutes

Ingredients:

- FOR THE JERK TOFU
- 1 (14-ounce) package extra-firm tofu, drained
- 1 tablespoon apple cider vinegar
- 1 tablespoon reduced-sodium soy sauce
- 2 tablespoons jerk seasoning
- Juice of 1 lime
- ½ teaspoon kosher salt
- 2 tablespoons olive oil
- FOR THE CABBAGE
- 1 (14-ounce) bag coleslaw mix
- 1 red bell pepper, thinly sliced
- 2 scallions, thinly sliced
- 2 tablespoons water
- 3 garlic cloves, minced
- ¼ teaspoon fresh thyme leaves
- ¼ teaspoon onion powder
- ¼ teaspoon kosher salt
- ¼ teaspoon freshly ground black pepper

Directions:

1. To prep the jerk tofu: Cut the tofu horizontally into 4 slabs.
2. In a shallow dish (big enough to hold the tofu slabs), whisk together the vinegar, soy sauce, jerk seasoning, lime juice, and salt.
3. Place the tofu in the marinade and turn to coat both sides. Cover and marinate for at least 15 minutes (or up to overnight in the refrigerator).
4. To prep the cabbage: In the Zone 2 basket, combine the coleslaw, bell pepper, scallions, water, garlic, thyme, onion powder, salt, and black pepper.
5. To cook the tofu and cabbage: Install a crisper plate in the Zone 1 basket and add the tofu in a single layer. Brush the tofu with the oil and insert the basket in the unit. Insert the Zone 2 basket in the unit.
6. Select Zone 1, select AIR FRY, set the temperature to 390°F, and set the timer to 15 minutes.
7. Select Zone 2, select ROAST, set the temperature to 330°F, and set the timer to 20 minutes. Select SMART FINISH.
8. Press START/PAUSE to begin cooking.
9. When both timers read 5 minutes, press START/PAUSE. Remove the Zone 1 basket and use silicone-tipped tongs to flip the tofu. Reinsert the basket in the unit. Remove the Zone 2 basket and stir the cabbage. Reinsert the basket and press START/PAUSE to resume cooking.
10. When cooking is complete, the tofu will be crispy and browned around the edges and the cabbage soft.
11. Transfer the tofu to four plates and serve with the cabbage on the side.

Nutrition Info:

- (Per serving) Calories: 220; Total fat: 12g; Saturated fat: 1.5g; Carbohydrates: 21g; Fiber: 5g; Protein: 12g; Sodium: 817mg

DESSERTS RECIPES

Desserts Recipes

Healthy Semolina Pudding

Servings: 4 | Cooking Time: 20 Minutes

Ingredients:

- 45g semolina
- 1 tsp vanilla
- 500ml milk
- 115g caster sugar

Directions:

1. Mix semolina and ½ cup milk in a bowl. Slowly add the remaining milk, sugar, and vanilla and mix well.
2. Pour the mixture into four greased ramekins.
3. Insert a crisper plate in the Ninja Foodi air fryer baskets.
4. Place ramekins in both baskets.
5. Select zone 1, then select "air fry" mode and set the temperature to 300 degrees F for 20 minutes. Press "match" to match zone 2 settings to zone 1. Press "start/stop" to begin.

Nutrition Info:

- (Per serving) Calories 209 | Fat 2.7g |Sodium 58mg | Carbs 41.5g | Fiber 0.6g | Sugar 30.6g | Protein 5.8g

Mocha Pudding Cake Vanilla Pudding Cake

Servings:8 | Cooking Time: 25 Minutes

Ingredients:

- FOR THE MOCHA PUDDING CAKE
- 1 cup all-purpose flour
- ⅔ cup granulated sugar
- 1 cup packed light brown sugar, divided
- 5 tablespoons unsweetened cocoa powder, divided
- 2 teaspoons baking powder
- ¼ teaspoon kosher salt
- ½ cup unsweetened almond milk
- 2 teaspoons vanilla extract
- 2 tablespoons vegetable oil
- 1 cup freshly brewed coffee
- FOR THE VANILLA PUDDING CAKE
- 1 cup all-purpose flour
- ⅔ cup granulated sugar, plus ½ cup
- 2 teaspoons baking powder
- ¼ teaspoon kosher salt
- ½ cup unsweetened almond milk
- 2½ teaspoons vanilla extract, divided
- 2 tablespoons vegetable oil
- ¾ cup hot water
- 2 teaspoons cornstarch

Directions:

1. To prep the mocha pudding cake: In a medium bowl, combine the flour, granulated sugar, ½ cup of brown sugar, 3 tablespoons of cocoa powder, the baking powder, and salt. Stir in the almond milk, vanilla, and oil to form a thick batter.
2. Spread the batter in the bottom of the Zone 1 basket. Sprinkle the remaining ½ cup brown sugar and 2 tablespoons of cocoa powder in an even layer over the batter. Gently pour the hot coffee over the batter (do not mix).
3. To prep the vanilla pudding cake: In a medium bowl, combine the flour, ⅔ cup of granulated sugar, the baking powder, and salt. Stir in the almond milk, 2 teaspoons of vanilla, and the oil to form a thick batter.
4. Spread the batter in the bottom of the Zone 2 basket.
5. In a small bowl, whisk together the hot water, cornstarch, and remaining ½ cup of sugar and ½ teaspoon of vanilla. Gently pour over the batter (do not mix).
6. To cook both pudding cakes: Insert both baskets in the unit.
7. Select Zone 1, select BAKE, set the temperature to 330°F, and set the timer to 25 minutes. Select MATCH COOK to match Zone 2 settings to Zone 1.
8. Press START/PAUSE to begin cooking.
9. When cooking is complete, the tops of the cakes should be dry and set.
10. Let the cakes rest for 10 minutes before serving. The pudding will thicken as it cools.

Nutrition Info:

- (Per serving) Calories: 531; Total fat: 8g; Saturated fat: 1g; Carbohydrates: 115g; Fiber: 3.5g; Protein: 5g; Sodium: 111mg

Cinnamon Sugar Dessert Fries

Servings: 4 | Cooking Time: 15 Minutes

Ingredients:

- 2 sweet potatoes
- 1 tablespoon butter, melted
- 1 teaspoon butter, melted
- 2 tablespoons sugar
- ½ teaspoon ground cinnamon

Directions:

1. Peel and cut the sweet potatoes into skinny fries.
2. Coat the fries with 1 tablespoon of butter.
3. Install a crisper plate into each drawer. Place half the sweet potatoes in the zone 1 drawer and half in zone 2's, then insert the drawers into the unit.
4. Select zone 1, select AIR FRY, set temperature to 390 degrees F/ 200 degrees C, and set time to 15 minutes. Select MATCH to match zone 2 settings to zone 1. Press the START/STOP button to begin cooking.
5. When the time reaches 11 minutes, press START/STOP to pause the unit. Remove the drawers and flip the fries. Re-insert the drawers into the unit and press START/STOP to resume cooking.
6. Meanwhile, mix the 1 teaspoon of butter, the sugar, and the cinnamon in a large bowl.
7. When the fries are done, add them to the bowl, and toss them to coat.
8. Serve and enjoy!

Nutrition Info:

- (Per serving) Calories 110 | Fat 4g | Sodium 51mg | Carbs 18g | Fiber 2g | Sugar 10g | Protein 1g

Cake In The Air Fryer

Servings:2 | Cooking Time:30

Ingredients:

- 90 grams all-purpose flour
- Pinch of salt
- 1/2 teaspoon of baking powder
- ½ cup of tutti fruitti mix
- 2 eggs
- 1 teaspoon of vanilla extract
- 10 tablespoons of white sugar

Directions:

1. Take a bowl and add all-purpose flour, salt, and baking powder.
2. Stir it in a large bowl.
3. Whisk two eggs in a separate bowl and add vanilla extract, sugar and blend it with a hand beater.
4. Now combine wet ingredients with the dry ones.
5. Mix it well and pour it between two round pan that fits inside baskets.
6. Place the pans in both the baskets.
7. Now set the zone 1 basket to BAKE function at 310 for 30 minutes.
8. Select MATCH for zone two baskets.
9. Once it's done, serve and enjoy.

Nutrition Info:

- (Per serving) Calories 711| Fat4.8g| Sodium 143mg | Carbs 161g | Fiber 1.3g | Sugar 105g | Protein 10.2g

Honey Lime Pineapple

Servings: 4 | Cooking Time: 10 Minutes

Ingredients:

- 562g pineapple chunks
- 55g brown sugar
- 30ml lime juice
- 63g honey

Directions:

1. In a bowl, mix pineapple, honey, lime juice, and brown sugar. Cover and place in refrigerator for 1 hour.
2. Insert a crisper plate in Ninja Foodi air fryer baskets.
3. Remove pineapple chunks from the marinade and place in both baskets.
4. Select zone 1 then select "air fry" mode and set the temperature to 390 degrees F for 10 minutes. Press "match" to match zone 2 settings to zone 1. Press "start/stop" to begin. Stir halfway through.

Nutrition Info:

- (Per serving) Calories 153 | Fat 0.2g |Sodium 5mg | Carbs 40.5g | Fiber 2g | Sugar 35.7g | Protein 0.8g

Fried Dough With Roasted Strawberries

Servings:4 | Cooking Time: 20 Minutes

Ingredients:

- FOR THE FRIED DOUGH
- 6 ounces refrigerated pizza dough, at room temperature
- 2 tablespoons all-purpose flour, for dusting
- 4 tablespoons vegetable oil
- 2 tablespoons powdered sugar
- FOR THE ROASTED STRAWBERRIES
- 2 cups frozen whole strawberries
- 2 tablespoons granulated sugar

Directions:

1. To prep the fried dough: Divide the dough into four equal portions.
2. Dust a clean work surface with the flour. Place one dough portion on the surface and use a rolling pin to roll to a ⅛-inch thickness. Rub both sides of the dough with 1 tablespoon of oil. Repeat with remaining dough portions and oil.
3. To prep the strawberries: Place the strawberries in the Zone 2 basket. Sprinkle the granulated sugar on top.

4. To cook the fried dough and strawberries: Install a crisper plate in the Zone 1 basket. Place 2 dough portions in the basket and insert the basket in the unit. Insert the Zone 2 basket in the unit.
5. Select Zone 1, select AIR FRY, set the temperature to 400°F, and set the timer to 18 minutes.
6. Select Zone 2, select ROAST, set the temperature to 330°F, and set the timer to 20 minutes. Select SMART FINISH.
7. Press START/PAUSE to begin cooking.
8. When both timers read 8 minutes, press START/PAUSE. Remove the Zone 1 basket and transfer the fried dough to a cutting board. Place the 2 remaining dough portions in the basket, then reinsert the basket. Remove the Zone 2 basket and stir the strawberries. Reinsert the basket and press START/PAUSE to resume cooking.
9. When cooking is complete, the dough should be cooked through and the strawberries soft and jammy.
10. Sprinkle the fried dough with powdered sugar. Gently mash the strawberries with a fork. Spoon the strawberries onto each fried dough portion and serve.

Nutrition Info:

- (Per serving) Calories: 304; Total fat: 15g; Saturated fat: 2.5g; Carbohydrates: 38g; Fiber: 0.5g; Protein: 3g; Sodium: 421mg

Walnut Baklava Bites Pistachio Baklava Bites

Servings:12 | Cooking Time: 10 Minutes

Ingredients:

- FOR THE WALNUT BAKLAVA BITES
- ¼ cup finely chopped walnuts
- 2 teaspoons cold unsalted butter, grated
- 2 teaspoons granulated sugar
- ½ teaspoon ground cinnamon
- 6 frozen phyllo shells (from a 1.9-ounce package), thawed
- FOR THE PISTACHIO BAKLAVA BITES
- ¼ cup finely chopped pistachios
- 2 teaspoons very cold unsalted butter, grated
- 2 teaspoons granulated sugar
- ¼ teaspoon ground cardamom (optional)
- 6 frozen phyllo shells (from a 1.9-ounce package), thawed
- FOR THE HONEY SYRUP
- ¼ cup hot water
- ¼ cup honey
- 2 teaspoons fresh lemon juice

Directions:

1. To prep the walnut baklava bites: In a small bowl, combine the walnuts, butter, sugar, and cinnamon. Spoon the filling into the phyllo shells.
2. To prep the pistachio baklava bites: In a small bowl, combine the pistachios, butter, sugar, and cardamom (if using). Spoon the filling into the phyllo shells.
3. To cook the baklava bites: Install a crisper plate in each of the two baskets. Place the walnut baklava bites in the Zone 1 basket and insert the basket in the unit. Place the pistachio baklava bites in the Zone 2 basket and insert the basket in the unit.
4. Select Zone 1, select BAKE, set the temperature to 330°F, and set the timer to 10 minutes. Press MATCH COOK to match Zone 2 settings to Zone 1.
5. Press START/PAUSE to begin cooking.
6. When cooking is complete, the shells will be golden brown and crisp.
7. To make the honey syrup: In a small bowl, whisk together the hot water, honey, and lemon juice. Dividing evenly, pour the syrup over the baklava bites (you may hear a crackling sound).
8. Let cool completely before serving, about 1 hour.

Nutrition Info:

- (Per serving) Calories: 262; Total fat: 16g; Saturated fat: 3g; Carbohydrates: 29g; Fiber: 1g; Protein: 2g; Sodium: 39mg

Apple Crumble Peach Crumble

Servings:8 | Cooking Time: 20 Minutes

Ingredients:

- FOR THE APPLE CRUMBLE
- ½ cup packed light brown sugar
- ¼ cup all-purpose flour
- ¼ cup rolled oats
- 2 tablespoons unsalted butter, at room temperature
- ½ teaspoon ground cinnamon
- ¼ teaspoon ground nutmeg
- ⅛ teaspoon kosher salt
- 4 medium Granny Smith apples, sliced
- FOR THE PEACH CRUMBLE
- ½ cup packed light brown sugar
- ¼ cup all-purpose flour
- ¼ cup rolled oats
- 2 tablespoons unsalted butter, at room temperature
- ½ teaspoon ground cinnamon
- ⅛ teaspoon kosher salt
- 4 peaches, peeled and sliced

Directions:

1. To prep the apple crumble: In a medium bowl,

combine the brown sugar, flour, oats, butter, cinnamon, nutmeg, and salt and mix well. The mixture will be dry and crumbly.

2. To prep the peach crumble: In a medium bowl, combine the brown sugar, flour, oats, butter, cinnamon, and salt and mix well. The mixture will be dry and crumbly.

3. To cook both crumbles: Spread the apples in the Zone 1 basket in an even layer. Top evenly with the apple crumble topping and insert the basket in the unit. Spread the peaches in the Zone 2 basket in an even layer. Top with the peach crumble topping and insert the basket in the unit.

4. Select Zone 1, select BAKE, set the temperature to 350°F, and set the timer to 20 minutes. Select MATCH COOK to match Zone 2 settings to Zone 1.

5. Press START/PAUSE to begin cooking.

6. When cooking is complete, the fruit will be tender and the crumble topping crisp and golden brown. Serve warm or at room temperature.

Nutrition Info:

- (Per serving) Calories: 300; Total fat: 6.5g; Saturated fat: 3.5g; Carbohydrates: 59g; Fiber: 5.5g; Protein: 2g; Sodium: 45mg

Pumpkin Muffins With Cinnamon

Servings: 4 | Cooking Time: 20 Minutes

Ingredients:

- 1 and ½ cups all-purpose flour
- ½ teaspoon baking soda
- ½ teaspoon baking powder
- 1 and ¼ teaspoons cinnamon, groaned
- ¼ teaspoon ground nutmeg, grated
- 2 large eggs
- Salt, pinch
- ¾ cup granulated sugar
- ½ cup dark brown sugar
- 1 and ½ cups pumpkin puree
- ¼ cup coconut milk

Directions:

1. Take 4 ramekins and layer them with muffin paper.
2. In a bowl, add the eggs, brown sugar, baking soda, baking powder, cinnamon, nutmeg, and sugar and whisk well with an electric mixer.
3. In a second bowl, mix the flour, and salt.
4. Slowly add the dry ingredients to the wet ingredients.
5. Fold in the pumpkin puree and milk and mix it in well.
6. Divide this batter into 4 ramekins.
7. Place two ramekins in each air fryer basket.
8. Set the time for zone 1 to 18 minutes at 360 degrees F/ 180 degrees C on AIR FRY mode.
9. Select the MATCH button for the zone 2 basket.
10. Check after the time is up and if not done, and let it AIR FRY for one more minute.
11. Once it is done, serve.

Nutrition Info:

- (Per serving) Calories 291 | Fat 6.4g | Sodium 241mg | Carbs 57.1g | Fiber 4.4g | Sugar 42g | Protein 5.9g

Fried Oreos

Servings: 8 | Cooking Time: 8 Minutes

Ingredients:

- 1 can Pillsbury Crescent Dough (or equivalent)
- 8 Oreo cookies
- 1–2 tablespoons powdered sugar

Directions:

1. Open the crescent dough up and cut it into the right-size pieces to completely wrap each cookie.
2. Wrap each Oreo in dough. Make sure that there are no air bubbles and that the cookies are completely covered.
3. Install a crisper plate in both drawers. Place half the Oreo cookies in the zone 1 drawer and half in zone 2's. Sprinkle the tops with the powdered sugar, then insert the drawers into the unit.
4. Select zone 1, select AIR FRY, set temperature to 390 degrees F/ 200 degrees C, and set time to 8 minutes. Select MATCH to match zone 2 settings to zone 1. Press the START/STOP button to begin cooking.
5. Serve warm and enjoy!

Nutrition Info:

- (Per serving) Calories 338 | Fat 21.2g | Sodium 1503mg | Carbs 5.1g | Fiber 0.3g | Sugar 4.6g | Protein 29.3g

Lava Cake

Servings: 4 | Cooking Time: 10 Minutes

Ingredients:

- 1 cup semi-sweet chocolate chips
- 8 tablespoons butter
- 4 eggs
- 2 teaspoons vanilla extract
- ½ teaspoon salt
- 6 tablespoons all-purpose flour
- 1 cup powdered sugar
- For the chocolate filling:
- 2 tablespoons Nutella
- 1 tablespoon butter, softened
- 1 tablespoon pow-

dered sugar

Directions:

1. Heat the chocolate chips and butter in a medium-sized microwave-safe bowl in 30-second intervals until thoroughly melted and smooth, stirring after each interval.
2. Whisk together the eggs, vanilla, salt, flour, and powdered sugar in a mixing bowl.
3. Combine the Nutella, softened butter, and powdered sugar in a separate bowl.
4. Spray 4 ramekins with oil and fill them halfway with the chocolate chip mixture. Fill each ramekin halfway with Nutella, then top with the remaining chocolate chip mixture, making sure the Nutella is well covered.
5. Install a crisper plate in both drawers. Place 2 ramekins in each drawer and insert the drawers into the unit.
6. Select zone 1, select AIR FRY, set temperature to 390 degrees F/ 200 degrees C, and set time to 22 minutes. Select MATCH to match zone 2 settings to zone 1. Press the START/STOP button to begin cooking.
7. Serve hot.

Nutrition Info:

- (Per serving) Calories 338 | Fat 21.2g | Sodium 1503mg | Carbs 5.1g | Fiber 0.3g | Sugar 4.6g | Protein 29.3g

Grilled Peaches

Servings: 2 | Cooking Time: 5 Minutes

Ingredients:

- 2 yellow peaches, peeled and cut into wedges
- ¼ cup graham cracker crumbs
- ¼ cup brown sugar
- ¼ cup butter diced into tiny cubes
- Whipped cream or ice cream

Directions:

1. Toss peaches with crumbs, brown sugar, and butter in a bowl.
2. Spread the peaches in one air fryer basket.
3. Return the air fryer basket to the Ninja Foodi 2 Baskets Air Fryer.
4. Choose the "Air Fry" mode for Zone 1 and set the temperature to 350 degrees F and 5 minutes of cooking time.
5. Initiate cooking by pressing the START/PAUSE BUTTON.
6. Serve the peaches with a scoop of ice cream.

Nutrition Info:

- (Per serving) Calories 327 | Fat 14.2g |Sodium 672mg | Carbs 47.2g | Fiber 1.7g | Sugar 24.8g | Protein 4.4g

Chocolate Pudding

Servings: 2 | Cooking Time: 12 Minutes

Ingredients:

- 1 egg
- 32g all-purpose flour
- 35g cocoa powder
- 50g sugar
- 57g butter, melted
- ½ tsp baking powder

Directions:

1. In a bowl, mix flour, cocoa powder, sugar, and baking powder.
2. Add egg and butter and stir until well combined.
3. Pour batter into the two greased ramekins.
4. Insert a crisper plate in Ninja Foodi air fryer baskets.
5. Place ramekins in both baskets.
6. Select zone 1 then select "bake" mode and set the temperature to 375 degrees F for 12 minutes. Press match cook to match zone 2 settings to zone 1. Press "start/stop" to begin.

Nutrition Info:

- (Per serving) Calories 512 | Fat 27.3g |Sodium 198mg | Carbs 70.6g | Fiber 4.7g | Sugar 50.5g | Protein 7.2g

Churros

Servings: 8 | Cooking Time: 10 Minutes

Ingredients:

- 1 cup water
- 1⁄3 cup unsalted butter, cut into cubes
- 2 tablespoons granulated sugar
- ¼ teaspoon salt
- 1 cup all-purpose flour
- 2 large eggs
- 1 teaspoon vanilla extract
- Cooking oil spray
- For the cinnamon-sugar coating:
- ½ cup granulated sugar
- ¾ teaspoon ground cinnamon

Directions:

1. Add the water, butter, sugar, and salt to a medium pot. Bring to a boil over medium-high heat.
2. Reduce the heat to medium-low and stir in the flour. Cook, stirring constantly with a rubber spatula until the dough is smooth and comes together.
3. Remove the dough from the heat and place it in a mixing bowl. Allow 4 minutes for cooling.

4. In a mixing bowl, beat the eggs and vanilla extract with an electric hand mixer or stand mixer until the dough comes together. The finished product will resemble gluey mashed potatoes. Press the lumps together into a ball with your hands, then transfer to a large piping bag with a large star-shaped tip. Pipe out the churros.
5. Install a crisper plate in both drawers. Place half the churros in the zone 1 drawer and half in zone 2's, then insert the drawers into the unit.
6. Select zone 1, select AIR FRY, set temperature to 390 degrees F/ 200 degrees C, and set time to 12 minutes. Select MATCH to match zone 2 settings to zone 1. Press the START/STOP button to begin cooking.
7. In a shallow bowl, combine the granulated sugar and cinnamon.
8. Immediately transfer the baked churros to the bowl with the sugar mixture and toss to coat.

Nutrition Info:

- (Per serving) Calories 204 | Fat 9g | Sodium 91mg | Carbs 27g | Fiber 0.3g | Sugar 15g | Protein 3g

Monkey Bread

Servings: 12 | Cooking Time: 10 Minutes

Ingredients:

- Bread
- 12 Rhodes white dinner rolls
- ½ cup brown sugar
- 1 teaspoon cinnamon
- 4 tablespoons butter melted
- Glaze
- ½ cup powdered sugar
- 1-2 tablespoons milk
- ½ teaspoon vanilla

Directions:

1. Mix brown sugar, cinnamon and butter in a bowl.
2. Cut the dinner rolls in half and dip them in the sugar mixture.
3. Place these buns in a greased baking pan and pour the remaining butter on top.
4. Place the buns in the air fryer baskets.
5. Return the air fryer basket 1 to Zone 1, and basket 2 to Zone 2 of the Ninja Foodi 2-Basket Air Fryer.
6. Choose the "Air Fry" mode for Zone 1 at 350 degrees F and 10 minutes of cooking time.
7. Initiate cooking by pressing the START/PAUSE BUTTON.
8. Flip the rolls once cooked halfway through.
9. Meanwhile, mix milk, vanilla and sugar in a bowl.
10. Pour the glaze over the air fried rolls.
11. Serve.

Nutrition Info:

- (Per serving) Calories 192 | Fat 9.3g |Sodium 133mg | Carbs 27.1g | Fiber 1.4g | Sugar 19g | Protein 3.2g

Apple Nutmeg Flautas

Servings: 8 | Cooking Time: 8 Minutes.

Ingredients:

- ¼ cup light brown sugar
- ⅛ cup all-purpose flour
- ¼ teaspoon ground cinnamon
- Nutmeg, to taste
- 4 apples, peeled, cored & sliced
- ½ lemon, juice, and zest
- 6 (10-inch) flour tortillas
- Vegetable oil
- Caramel sauce
- Cinnamon sugar

Directions:

1. Mix brown sugar with cinnamon, nutmeg, and flour in a large bowl.
2. Toss in apples in lemon juice. Mix well.
3. Place a tortilla at a time on a flat surface and add ½ cup of the apple mixture to the tortilla.
4. Roll the tortilla into a burrito and seal it tightly and hold it in place with a toothpick.
5. Repeat the same steps with the remaining tortillas and apple mixture.
6. Place two apple burritos in each of the crisper plate and spray them with cooking oil.
7. Return the crisper plates to the Ninja Foodi Dual Zone Air Fryer.
8. Choose the Air Fry mode for Zone 1 and set the temperature to 400 degrees F and the time to 8 minutes.
9. Select the "MATCH" button to copy the settings for Zone 2.
10. Initiate cooking by pressing the START/STOP button.
11. Flip the burritos once cooked halfway through, then resume cooking.
12. Garnish with caramel sauce and cinnamon sugar.
13. Enjoy!

Nutrition Info:

- (Per serving) Calories 157 | Fat 1.3g |Sodium 27mg | Carbs 1.3g | Fiber 1g | Sugar 2.2g | Protein 8.2g

Chocó Lava Cake

Servings: 4 | Cooking Time: 10 Minutes

Ingredients:

- 3 eggs
- 3 egg yolks
- 70g dark chocolate, chopped
- 168g cups powdered sugar
- 96g all-purpose flour
- 1 tsp vanilla
- 113g butter
- ½ tsp salt

Directions:

1. Add chocolate and butter to a bowl and microwave for 30 seconds. Remove from oven and stir until smooth.
2. Add eggs, egg yolks, sugar, flour, vanilla, and salt into the melted chocolate and stir until well combined.
3. Pour batter into the four greased ramekins.
4. Insert a crisper plate in Ninja Foodi air fryer baskets.
5. Place ramekins in both baskets.
6. Select zone 1 then select "air fry" mode and set the temperature to 390 degrees F for 10 minutes. Press "match" to match zone 2 settings to zone 1. Press "start/stop" to begin.

Nutrition Info:

- (Per serving) Calories 687 | Fat 37.3g |Sodium 527mg | Carbs 78.3g | Fiber 1.5g | Sugar 57.4g | Protein 10.7g

Baked Apples

Servings: 4 | Cooking Time: 15 Minutes

Ingredients:

- 4 apples
- 6 teaspoons raisins
- 2 teaspoons chopped walnuts
- 2 teaspoons honey
- ½ teaspoon cinnamon

Directions:

1. Chop off the head of the apples and scoop out the flesh from the center.
2. Stuff the apples with raisins, walnuts, honey and cinnamon.
3. Place these apples in the air fryer basket 1.
4. Return the air fryer basket 1 to Zone 1 of the Ninja Foodi 2-Basket Air Fryer.
5. Choose the "Air Fry" mode for Zone 1 and set the temperature to 350 degrees F and 15 minutes of cooking time.
6. Initiate cooking by pressing the START/PAUSE BUTTON.
7. Serve.

Nutrition Info:

- (Per serving) Calories 175 | Fat 13.1g |Sodium 154mg | Carbs 14g | Fiber 0.8g | Sugar 8.9g | Protein 0.7g

Dehydrated Peaches

Servings: 4 | Cooking Time: 8 Hours

Ingredients:

- 300g canned peaches

Directions:

1. Insert a crisper plate in the Ninja Foodi air fryer baskets.
2. Place peaches in both baskets.
3. Select zone 1, then select "dehydrate" mode and set the temperature to 135 degrees F for 8 hours. Press "start/stop" to begin.

Nutrition Info:

- (Per serving) Calories 30 | Fat 0.2g |Sodium 0mg | Carbs 7g | Fiber 1.2g | Sugar 7g | Protein 0.7g

Apple Fritters

Servings: 14 | Cooking Time: 10 Minutes

Ingredients:

- 2 large apples
- 2 cups all-purpose flour
- ½ cup granulated sugar
- 1 tablespoon baking powder
- 1 teaspoon salt
- 1 teaspoon ground cinnamon
- ½ teaspoon ground nutmeg
- ¼ teaspoon ground cloves
- ¾ cup apple cider or apple juice
- 2 eggs
- 3 tablespoons butter, melted
- 1 teaspoon vanilla extract
- For the apple cider glaze:
- 2 cups powdered sugar
- ¼ cup apple cider or apple juice
- ½ teaspoon ground cinnamon
- ¼ teaspoon ground nutmeg

Directions:

1. Peel and core the apples, then cut them into ¼-inch cubes. Spread the apple chunks out on a kitchen towel to absorb any excess moisture.
2. In a mixing bowl, combine the flour, sugar, baking powder, salt, and spices.
3. Add the apple chunks and combine well.
4. Whisk together the apple cider, eggs, melted butter, and vanilla in a small bowl.
5. Combine the wet and dry ingredients in a large mixing bowl.

6. Install a crisper plate in both drawers. Use an ice cream scoop to scoop 3 to 4 dollops of fritter dough into the zone 1 drawer and 3 to 4 dollops into the zone 2 drawer. Insert the drawers into the unit. You may need to cook in batches.
7. Select zone 1, select BAKE, set temperature to 390 degrees F/ 200 degrees C, and set time to 10 minutes. Select MATCH to match zone 2 settings to zone 1. Press the START/STOP button to begin cooking.
8. Meanwhile, make the glaze: Whisk the powdered sugar, apple cider, and spices together until smooth.
9. When the fritters are cooked, drizzle the glaze over them. Let sit for 10 minutes until the glaze sets.

Nutrition Info:

- (Per serving) Calories 221 | Fat 3g | Sodium 288mg | Carbs 46g | Fiber 2g | Sugar 29g | Protein 3g

Jelly Donuts

Servings: 4 | Cooking Time: 5 Minutes

Ingredients:

- 1 package Pillsbury Grands (Homestyle)
- ½ cup seedless raspberry jelly
- 1 tablespoon butter, melted
- ½ cup sugar

Directions:

1. Install a crisper plate in both drawers. Place half of the biscuits in the zone 1 drawer and half in zone 2's, then insert the drawers into the unit. You may need to cook in batches.
2. Select zone 1, select AIR FRY, set temperature to 390 degrees F/ 200 degrees C, and set time to 22 minutes. Select MATCH to match zone 2 settings to zone 1. Press the START/STOP button to begin cooking.
3. Place the sugar into a wide bowl with a flat bottom.
4. Baste all sides of the cooked biscuits with the melted butter and roll in the sugar to cover completely.
5. Using a long cake tip, pipe 1–2 tablespoons of raspberry jelly into each biscuit. You've now got raspberry-filled donuts!

Nutrition Info:

- (Per serving) Calories 252 | Fat 7g | Sodium 503mg | Carbs 45g | Fiber 0g | Sugar 23g | Protein 3g

Biscuit Doughnuts

Servings: 8 | Cooking Time: 15 Minutes.

Ingredients:

- ½ cup white sugar
- 1 teaspoon cinnamon
- ½ cup powdered sugar
- 1 can pre-made biscuit dough
- Coconut oil
- Melted butter to brush biscuits

Directions:

1. Place all the biscuits on a cutting board and cut holes in the center of each biscuit using a cookie cutter.
2. Grease the crisper plate with coconut oil.
3. Place the biscuits in the two crisper plates while keeping them 1 inch apart.
4. Return the crisper plates to the Ninja Foodi Dual Zone Air Fryer.
5. Choose the Air Fry mode for Zone 1 and set the temperature to 375 degrees F and the time to 15 minutes.
6. Select the "MATCH" button to copy the settings for Zone 2.
7. Initiate cooking by pressing the START/STOP button.
8. Brush all the donuts with melted butter and sprinkle cinnamon and sugar on top.
9. Air fry these donuts for one minute more.
10. Enjoy!

Nutrition Info:

- (Per serving) Calories 192 | Fat 9.3g |Sodium 133mg | Carbs 27.1g | Fiber 1.4g | Sugar 19g | Protein 3.2g

Chocolate Cookies

Servings: 18 | Cooking Time: 7 Minutes

Ingredients:

- 96g flour
- 57g butter, softened
- 15ml milk
- 7.5g cocoa powder
- 80g chocolate chips
- ½ tsp vanilla
- 35g sugar
- ¼ tsp baking soda
- Pinch of salt

Directions:

1. In a bowl, mix flour, cocoa powder, sugar, baking soda, vanilla, butter, milk, and salt until well combined.
2. Add chocolate chips and mix well.
3. Insert a crisper plate in Ninja Foodi air fryer baskets.
4. Make cookies from the mixture and place in both

baskets.

5. Select zone 1 then select "air fry" mode and set the temperature to 360 degrees F for 7 minutes. Press "match" to match zone 2 settings to zone 1. Press "start/stop" to begin.

Nutrition Info:

- (Per serving) Calories 82 | Fat 4.1g |Sodium 47mg | Carbs 10.7g | Fiber 0.4g | Sugar 6.2g | Protein 1g

Dessert Empanadas

Servings: 12 | Cooking Time: 10 Minutes

Ingredients:

- 12 empanada wrappers thawed
- 2 apples, chopped
- 2 tablespoons raw honey
- 1 teaspoon vanilla extract
- 1 teaspoon cinnamon
- ⅛ teaspoon nutmeg
- 2 teaspoons cornstarch
- 1 teaspoon water
- 1 egg beaten

Directions:

1. Mix apples with vanilla, honey, nutmeg, and cinnamon in a saucepan.
2. Cook for 3 minutes then mix cornstarch with water and pour into the pan.
3. Cook for 30 seconds.
4. Allow this filling to cool and keep it aside.
5. Spread the wrappers on the working surface.
6. Divide the apple filling on top of the wrappers.
7. Fold the wrappers in half and seal the edges by pressing them.
8. Brush the empanadas with the beaten egg and place them in the air fryer basket 1.
9. Return the air fryer basket 1 to Zone 1 of the Ninja Foodi 2-Basket Air Fryer.
10. Choose the "Air Fry" mode for Zone 1 at 400 degrees F and 10 minutes of cooking time.
11. Initiate cooking by pressing the START/PAUSE BUTTON.
12. Flip the empanadas once cooked halfway through.
13. Serve.

Nutrition Info:

- (Per serving) Calories 204 | Fat 9g |Sodium 91mg | Carbs 27g | Fiber 2.4g | Sugar 15g | Protein 1.3g

Pumpkin Muffins

Servings:4 | Cooking Time:20

Ingredients:

- 1 and ½ cups of all-purpose flour
- ½ teaspoon baking soda
- ½ teaspoon of baking powder
- 1 and 1/4 teaspoons cinnamon, groaned
- 1/4 teaspoon ground nutmeg, grated
- 2 large eggs
- Salt, pinch
- 3/4 cup granulated sugar
- 1/2 cup dark brown sugar
- 1 and 1/2 cups of pumpkin puree
- 1/4 cup coconut milk

Directions:

1. Take 4 ramekins that are the size of a cup and layer them with muffin papers.
2. Crack an egg in a bowl and add brown sugar, baking soda, baking powder, cinnamon, nutmeg, and sugar.
3. Whisk it all very well with an electric hand beater.
4. Now, in a second bowl, mix the flour, and salt.
5. Now, mix the dry ingredients slowly with the wet ingredients.
6. Now, at the end fold in the pumpkin puree and milk, mix it well
7. Divide this batter into 4 ramekins.
8. Now, divide ramekins between both zones.
9. Set the time for zone 1 to 18 minutes at 360 degrees Fat AIRFRY mode.
10. Select the MATCH button for the zone 2 basket.
11. Check if not done, and let it AIR FRY for one more minute.
12. Once it is done, serve.

Nutrition Info:

- (Per serving) Calories 291| Fat6.4 g| Sodium 241mg | Carbs 57.1g | Fiber 4.4g | Sugar42 g | Protein 5.9g

S'mores Dip With Cinnamon-sugar Tortillas

Servings:4 | Cooking Time: 5 Minutes

Ingredients:

- FOR THE S'MORES DIP
- ½ cup chocolate-hazelnut spread
- ¼ cup milk chocolate or white chocolate chips
- ¼ cup graham cracker crumbs
- ½ cup mini marshmallows
- FOR THE CINNAMON-SUGAR TORTILLAS
- 4 (6-inch) flour tortillas
- Butter-flavored cooking spray
- 1 teaspoon granulated sugar
- ½ teaspoon ground cinnamon
- ¼ teaspoon ground cardamom (optional)

Directions:

1. To prep the s'mores dip: Spread the chocolate-hazelnut spread in the bottom of a shallow ovenproof ramekin or dish.
2. Scatter the chocolate chips and graham cracker crumbs over the top. Arrange the marshmallows in a single layer on top of the crumbs.
3. To prep the tortillas: Spray both sides of each tortilla with cooking spray. Cut each tortilla into 8 wedges and sprinkle both sides evenly with sugar, cinnamon, and cardamom (if using).
4. To cook the dip and tortillas: Install a crisper plate in each of the two baskets. Place the ramekin in the Zone 1 basket and insert the basket in the unit. Place the tortillas in the Zone 2 basket and insert the basket in the unit.
5. Select Zone 1, select BAKE, set the temperature to 330°F, and set the timer to 5 minutes.
6. Select Zone 2, select AIR FRY, set the temperature to 375°F, and set the timer to 5 minutes. Select SMART FINISH.
7. Press START/PAUSE to begin cooking.
8. When the Zone 2 timer reads 3 minutes, press START/PAUSE. Remove the basket and shake it to redistribute the chips. Reinsert the basket and press START/PAUSE to resume cooking.
9. When cooking is complete, the dip will be bubbling and golden brown and the chips crispy.
10. If desired, toast the marshmallows more: Select Zone 1, select AIR BROIL, set the temperature to 450°F, and set the timer to 1 minute. Cook until the marshmallows are deep golden brown.
11. Let the dip cool for 2 to 3 minutes. Serve with the cinnamon-sugar tortilla chips.

Nutrition Info:

- (Per serving) Calories: 404; Total fat: 18g; Saturated fat: 7g; Carbohydrates: 54g; Fiber: 2.5g; Protein: 6g; Sodium: 346mg

Recipe

From the kicthen of

Serves . . . . Prep time . . . . Cook time . . . .

- [ ] Difficulty
- [ ] Easy
- [ ] Medium
- [ ] Hard

Ingredient

Directions

Date: ____________________

MY SHOPPING LIST

APPENDIX A: Measurement Conversions

BASIC KITCHEN CONVERSIONS & EQUIVALENTS

DRY MEASUREMENTS CONVERSION CHART

3 TEASPOONS = 1 TABLESPOON = 1/16 CUP

6 TEASPOONS = 2 TABLESPOONS = 1/8 CUP

12 TEASPOONS = 4 TABLESPOONS = 1/4 CUP

24 TEASPOONS = 8 TABLESPOONS = 1/2 CUP

36 TEASPOONS = 12 TABLESPOONS = 3/4 CUP

48 TEASPOONS = 16 TABLESPOONS = 1 CUP

METRIC TO US COOKING CONVERSIONS

OVEN TEMPERATURES

120 °C = 250 °F

160 °C = 320 °F

180° C = 350 °F

205 °C = 400 °F

220 °C = 425 °F

LIQUID MEASUREMENTS CONVERSION CHART

8 FLUID OUNCES = 1 CUP = 1/2 PINT = 1/4 QUART

16 FLUID OUNCES = 2 CUPS = 1 PINT = 1/2 QUART

32 FLUID OUNCES = 4 CUPS = 2 PINTS = 1 QUART

= 1/4 GALLON

128 FLUID OUNCES = 16 CUPS = 8 PINTS = 4 QUARTS = 1 GALLON

BAKING IN GRAMS

1 CUP FLOUR = 140 GRAMS

1 CUP SUGAR = 150 GRAMS

1 CUP POWDERED SUGAR = 160 GRAMS

1 CUP HEAVY CREAM = 235 GRAMS

VOLUME

1 MILLILITER = 1/5 TEASPOON

5 ML = 1 TEASPOON

15 ML = 1 TABLESPOON

240 ML = 1 CUP OR 8 FLUID OUNCES

1 LITER = 34 FL. OUNCES

WEIGHT

1 GRAM = .035 OUNCES

100 GRAMS = 3.5 OUNCES

500 GRAMS = 1.1 POUNDS

1 KILOGRAM = 35 OUNCES

US TO METRIC COOKING CONVERSIONS

1/5 TSP = 1 ML

1 TSP = 5 ML

1 TBSP = 15 ML

1 FL OUNCE = 30 ML

1 CUP = 237 ML

1 PINT (2 CUPS) = 473 ML

1 QUART (4 CUPS) = .95 LITER

1 GALLON (16 CUPS) = 3.8 LITERS

1 OZ = 28 GRAMS

1 POUND = 454 GRAMS

BUTTER

1 CUP BUTTER = 2 STICKS = 8 OUNCES = 230 GRAMS = 8 TABLESPOONS

WHAT DOES 1 CUP EQUAL

1 CUP = 8 FLUID OUNCES

1 CUP = 16 TABLESPOONS

1 CUP = 48 TEASPOONS

1 CUP = 1/2 PINT

1 CUP = 1/4 QUART

1 CUP = 1/16 GALLON

1 CUP = 240 ML

BAKING PAN CONVERSIONS

1 CUP ALL-PURPOSE FLOUR = 4.5 OZ

1 CUP ROLLED OATS = 3 OZ 1 LARGE EGG = 1.7 OZ

1 CUP BUTTER = 8 OZ 1 CUP MILK = 8 OZ

1 CUP HEAVY CREAM = 8.4 OZ

1 CUP GRANULATED SUGAR = 7.1 OZ

1 CUP PACKED BROWN SUGAR = 7.75 OZ

1 CUP VEGETABLE OIL = 7.7 OZ

1 CUP UNSIFTED POWDERED SUGAR = 4.4 OZ

BAKING PAN CONVERSIONS

9-INCH ROUND CAKE PAN = 12 CUPS

10-INCH TUBE PAN =16 CUPS

11-INCH BUNDT PAN = 12 CUPS

9-INCH SPRINGFORM PAN = 10 CUPS

9 X 5 INCH LOAF PAN = 8 CUPS

9-INCH SQUARE PAN = 8 CUPS

Appendix B : Recipes Index

A

B

C

D

J

K

L

M

O

P

Q

R

S

Printed in Great Britain
by Amazon

35436163R00057